WISDOM
FOR OUR
WORRIES

Also by Bill Crowder

Before Christmas

For This He Came

God of Surprise

Gospel on the Mountains

Let's Talk

Moving beyond Failure

My Hope Is in You

One Thing Is Necessary

Overcoming Life's Challenges

Seeing the Heart of Christ

The Spotlight of Faith

Trusting God in Hard Times

Windows on Christmas

Windows on Easter

Devotionals

A Compassionate Heart

A Present Peace

WISDOM
FOR OUR
WORRIES

Finding Joy and Peace
in Difficult Times

BILL
CROWDER

Our Daily Bread
Publishing.

Wisdom for Our Worries: Finding Joy and Peace in Difficult Times
© 2023 by William Crowder

Cover and Interior design by Michael J. Williams

Library of Congress Cataloging-in-Publication Data

Names: Crowder, Bill, author.
Title: Wisdom for our worries : find joy and peace in difficult times / Bill Crowder.
Description: Grand Rapids, MI : Our Daily Bread Publishing, [2023] | Summary: ""Bill Crowder breaks down the topic of fear using examples from the lives of Bible heroes to help readers understand how God's faithfulness in the past makes it easier to face the anxieties of the future"--Provided by publisher"-- Provided by publisher.
Identifiers: LCCN 2022049530 (print) | LCCN 2022049531 (ebook) | ISBN 9781640702172 | ISBN 9781640702493 (ebook)
Subjects: LCSH: Worry--Religious aspects--Christianity. | Peace of mind--Religious aspects--Christianity.
Classification: LCC BV4908.5 .C767 2023 (print) | LCC BV4908.5 (ebook) | DDC 248.8/6--dc23/eng/20230126
LC record available at https://lccn.loc.gov/2022049530
LC ebook record available at https://lccn.loc.gov/2022049531

Printed in the United States of America

23 24 25 26 27 28 29 30 / 9 8 7 6 5 4 3 2

For trusted helpers who made sure I had less to worry about: Betsy Garrett, Patty Block, Carol (Tien) Winslow, Melissa Monk, Katy Pent

CONTENTS

Acknowledgments   9

Introduction: But, What If . . . ?   11

1. The Elephant in the Room   15

2. Cause and Effect   33

3. Professional Worrying: Bible Style   51

4. Singing Our Worries and Anxieties   71

5. Speaking Words of Wisdom   87

6. Walls to Lean On   103

Conclusion: The Who Is the Why . . .   119

ACKNOWLEDGMENTS

When I was asked to write a book about worry, I had to admit somewhat grudgingly that I am probably an expert on the subject. Not in a good or theoretical way, but in a practical way. I have spent much of my life battling with worry for a variety of reasons. So, as I dove into this project, it was with a sense of anticipation. It was (and is) my sincere desire that this book will be of help and encouragement to you—the reader. But it was also my hope that it would be of help to me. Worry is just not a healthy place to be. I say that even as I acknowledge my own propensity to worry and fret.

I want to say a big thank-you to the team at Our Daily Bread Publishing. Knowing that worry is one subject that overtakes many of us, it feels like I have been given a trust to speak to such a complex and thorny issue. I am grateful to Chriscynethia Floyd, Dawn Anderson, Anna Haggard, Katara Patton, and Joel Armstrong (my stalwart editor) for their support, encouragement, and graciousness during the rather bumpy process of producing this book. I also want to thank Marjie Johnson and the marketing team for their suggestion of the topic and their faithful work that has helped this book arrive safely into your hands. As I have said before, I am deeply grateful to work with a first-class publisher that is staffed by men and women I count as friends.

I continue to be amazed at the patience and resiliency of my wonderful wife, Marlene. Her gentle encouragement and prodding kept me going when the writing process became long and difficult. Writing isn't easy—especially when the words don't flow. Seeking to go that extra mile to do my best, I felt the little nudges she offered as a great help in bringing this manuscript to a form that I was comfortable with submitting. Though they are now out of the house and we have an empty nest, our kids (and grandkids) continue to be a great source of joy and inspiration. I am so deeply thankful for my family—including my parents, who are now both with the Lord, and my siblings, three of whom have also gone to be with Jesus. How anybody does anything alone is beyond me. I am grateful for every cheerleader and encourager God gives me.

Finally, I am grateful to my God—who is in control, even when my worrying might suggest otherwise. He is truly a good, good Father who is trustworthy. That reality, by itself, reveals how unnecessary and foolish worry really is.

INTRODUCTION
But, What If . . . ?

Worry does not empty tomorrow of its sorrow,
it empties today of its strength.

—Corrie ten Boom

Worry has an endless amount of fuel in our generation (and apparently other generations as well), yet the Scriptures challenge us to move beyond worry. How? And why is it so hard?

Corrie ten Boom, whose words preface this introduction, offers us a point of wisdom that is easy to agree with and hard to live out. And, it is my guess at least, Corrie wasn't born with that understanding. It was a wisdom learned in one of life's most unimaginable experiences—attempting to survive in a Nazi death camp.

Anyone familiar with Corrie's story, told in *The Hiding Place*, knows the background. With the rise of anti-Semitism in 1930s Europe, the Ten Boom family decided to make a difference. They created a literal hiding place behind a cupboard area in their little apartment home over top of Mr. Ten Boom's watch shop in Amsterdam, Netherlands, as a place to protect Jews who were trying to escape the Nazis' "final solution to the Jewish question." The place was tiny, holding six adults standing in a row, and anytime there were people in the hiding place, the entire household must have been thick with anxiety.

Some years ago, Corrie's story from the somewhat distant past became very much alive to me. I was leading a study group to Israel, and on the travel over from the States we had a daylong stopover in Amsterdam, so I scheduled us a tour of the city. Among other things, we saw the Anne Frank house and spent a fair bit of time in the Ten Boom residence—the living room still looking as it did the night the family was arrested. We saw the hiding place and some of our group squirmed their way in to feel the experience.

As I stood there looking at my friends in that very special place, it was not hard to imagine the stress levels in that little home. Wondering when the next batch of escapees might arrive. Wondering how they could keep them safe. Wondering if the next knock on the door would be the Gestapo. And, it seemed to me, it would be a very easy thing for the wondering to turn into worrying. Especially after the day that the next knock on the door was the Gestapo and the Ten Boom family was hauled away to prison. Corrie's father, Casper, died soon after the arrest, and she and her sister, Betsie, eventually arrived at the Ravensbrück concentration camp.

In the camp, every day was another exercise in survival as they wondered what would happen next. Betsie died in the camp, but Corrie survived. She went on to be a marvelous representative of a forgiving heart and a faithful follower of Jesus.

But I am struck by her comment. See it again:

> Worry does not empty tomorrow of its sorrow, it empties today of its strength.

Admittedly, most of the worries that plague me do not rise to the level of anxiety the Ten Boom family surely knew. But from the depths of her experience I was able to embrace the wisdom of her words about worry. If anyone's life had reason to be grounded in worry and anxiety, it was Corrie ten Boom's, yet she learned a better way. A way of faith and hope. A way not learned in a laboratory. A way not learned in a classroom. A way learned though experiencing life's most brutal possibilities. A way that echoes the spiritual corrective found in the hymn "Great Is Thy Faithfulness," which reminds us that, in our faithful God, we can find

> strength for today and bright hope for tomorrow.

The contrast is remarkable—and very, very real. Our faithful God is the ultimate counterpoint to worry, both today and tomorrow. Join me as we explore together both the problem of worry and the God who is greater than all our worries.

Chapter One

THE ELEPHANT
IN THE ROOM

Worry often gives a small thing a big shadow.
—Swedish Proverb

As I write this, war is raging in eastern Europe—the result of Russia invading Ukraine. The entire global community, it seems, has felt the anxieties generated by this unprovoked conflict. That raging conflagration has taken thousands of innocent lives and destroyed billions of dollars of property. With Europe engulfed in fear of that war spreading to other countries, I found that it was a fear to which I could relate.

As a child growing up in the United States of America, I was taught to hate Russia and, even more, to fear them as a nation. Then, in the mid-1990s, following the collapse of the Soviet Union, an extraordinary door of opportunity for ministry opened as Russian believers began reaching out with the good news of Jesus and planting churches with the new Christ followers that were coming to faith. The fly in the buttermilk was that there were very few people who had pastoral training to serve those congregations. As a result, some of us from the States traveled to Russia to offer teaching in Bible, theology, preaching, and shepherding. This unprecedented opportunity, however, also carried with it a significant challenge—as a child of the Cold War, for my first trip outside North America, I was going to be there. *In Russia.* Among people I had been taught to hate, fear, and distrust my whole life. Daunting.

The first Russian I saw was a soldier carrying an AK-47 automatic rifle (gulp). My first day in Moscow I was taken to the Kremlin. The foreignness of everything was unsettling and, for me, a constant weight that threatened to knock me totally off-balance. As a result, I wondered (read *worried*) about almost everything. Every day I peppered the school's staff with dozens of questions about everything I was uncomfortable with. Which, well, was pretty much everything. One of the office staff, a dear lady named Tamara Platova (who over the years would become my Moscow "mom"), was the target of the lion's share of those questions. She would listen patiently, respond understandingly, and allay my worries for another moment. Then after several days, as I once again unloaded a barrage of questions on her, Tamara finally smiled and said in her thickly accented English, "Beeeulll [that would be *Bill*], do not vorry." I tried to smile back and appear casual as I responded, "Tamara, I am not worried—I am only concerned."

But Tamara knew better. And so did I. My worries were morphing into anxieties that could only disrupt any effectiveness I might have in working with my students. And, frankly, it wasn't doing my digestive system any good either.

Certainly our world is dangerous. Unpredictable. Filled with unknowns. Many of our major cities are places of great violence, yet even small towns can feel the heartache of gun violence against the most vulnerable of us—our children. Unanticipated diseases and health dangers arise seemingly from nowhere to threaten our well-being. Inflation assaults the economy, raising prices while incomes plateau. We look at the instability of our time and wonder, What kind of world are we leaving to our kids? Our grandkids? These very real fear triggers, and dozens of others, have caused more than a few sleepless nights. And this isn't the by-product of an overactive imagination. These fears are legitimate.

Yet, though it is often our response to those realities, worry is incapable of addressing or resolving any of the life factors that tend to provoke it. Worry is both diminishing and destructive because it focuses our hearts and minds on thousands of possible circumstances while pulling our hearts and minds away from the kind of confidence in God that can enable us to live in the abundance of life Jesus offers us (John 10:10).

It is far too easy to welcome worry as a familiar friend when, in fact, it is one of the most profound enemies of our walk of faith.

All of Us Worry

Worry has been described as giving way to anxiety—dwelling on fears or troubles to the point of anxiety. And we all do it at one time or another. For some, it is just that bit of unsettledness that nags at the back of our minds about a situation. For others, it is much more serious, swelling into what is known clinically as generalized anxiety disorder (GAD). The National Institute of Mental Health explains the dynamics of GAD this way:

> Occasional anxiety is a normal part of life. Many people may worry about things such as health, money, or family problems. But people with GAD feel extremely worried or nervous more frequently about these and other things—even when there is little or no reason to worry about them. GAD usually involves a persistent feeling of anxiety or dread that interferes with how you live your life.

Which, to me, sounds very much like my first Moscow experience. However, whether it falls into the category of occasional anxiety or the more serious generalized anxiety disorder, worry is a universal problem—and part of the human experience. A *Washington Post* survey reported in 2020 that 60 percent of US adults struggle with worry on a daily basis. That is a shocking statistic when you take into account the *HuffPost* study that posited that

85 percent of the things we worry about *never happen*. This stat underlines the message of the Swedish proverb that opened this chapter:

> Worry often gives a small thing a big shadow.

As people who are called to walk in the light as Jesus is in the light (1 John 1:7), living within the dark shadows of worry not only is counterproductive but can be spiritually debilitating. Worry wears us down. Yet, while we know that, it is much easier to state the dangers of worry in terms of fact than it is to deal with the issue of worry. Many of the things we worry about are tangible. Worry itself is amorphous. There is no on-off switch. There is no vaccine. There is no formula. It is this very intangibility that makes worry such a fierce enemy.

When my kids were younger, the boys enjoyed watching G. I. Joe cartoons. They would watch Duke or Snake Eyes or some other hero battling evil and—of course—winning. But, at the end of each episode, there was a closing moment which focused on some life fact or personal living tip. After some bit of knowledge was shared, that episode's final feature would conclude with G. I. Joe sagely intoning, "Now you know, and knowing is half the battle."

That assertion may be somewhat overstated, but knowledge can at least help us to be better equipped to do battle with the worries and anxieties that dog our hearts. And it starts with understanding our foe. So then, at its core, what is worry all about?

Two Kinds of Worry

Many of us are familiar with the statement that often opens a conversation, "I've got good news and I've got bad news. Which do you want first?" When it comes to understanding, as a follower of Christ, the nature of worry, I'm afraid I have bad news and bad news.

There seems to be an unlimited number of things to worry about, and yet, at the risk of sounding simplistic, most if not all of those infinite possibilities fall into two areas of bad news for the child of God. A paraphrase of a wise statement from pastor and church leader Tim Keller offers us those two categories:

Doubt is fearing that God got it wrong.
Anxiety is fearing that God won't get it right.

One kind of worry is anchored to the past while the other struggles with the future, and in both cases the trustworthiness of God is questioned. What makes this so important is that, while these two forms are focused on the past and the future, they can have a profound effect on how we live in the present. Worry—whether in the form of doubt or anxiety—is the opposite of authentic trust in God, and that is a major problem for people who are called by the Scriptures to live by faith (Galatians 2:20).

So, since knowing is half the battle, what do we need to know about both doubt and anxiety?

Doubt. In the earliest moments of human history, doubt was at the root of our first parents' failure. In their

Edenic home, Adam and Eve had full and complete provision for every aspect of life: unhindered communion with God, a perfect environment, an abundant supply of food, meaningful work, and a relationship with one another that was the very definition of bliss. As the old song (and more recent car commercials) said, "Who could ask for anything more?"

As a result, when the Enemy sought to bring disruption into the garden of perfection, he didn't do it by interjecting want or suggesting a lack of anything. He did it by introducing doubt. "Has God really said . . . ?" (Genesis 3:1). Could they really trust God's words? God's provision? God's care? In other words, the Enemy was probing Eve's innocence and naivete with the question, "Are you really sure God got it right?" By generating doubt about God and His provision, the Serpent created the first moment of worry.

What if . . . ?

This continues to be one of the core elements of worry for the child of God. We see that same kind of doubt reflected in the children of Israel in the wilderness. Having just experienced the powerful intervention of God that delivered them from four centuries of Egyptian bondage through miraculous displays of divine might on their behalf, they had barely begun their travels into the wilderness when they voiced their doubts about God's purposes:

> The whole congregation of the sons of Israel grumbled against Moses and Aaron in the wilderness. The sons of Israel said to

them, "If only we had died by the Lord's hand in the land of Egypt, when we sat by the pots of meat, when we ate bread until we were full; for you have brought us out into this wilderness to kill this entire assembly with hunger!" (Exodus 16:2–3)

Do you hear it? It is as if they are asking, "What was God thinking? We were fine in Egypt. Lots of food, plenty of provision. I mean, yeah, we were slaves and all, but at least we got fed. Why didn't God just leave us there? God has brought us to freedom, but what does that matter if we starve out here in the wilderness? Wouldn't we have been better off in Egypt?"

Which being interpreted means, "Did God get it wrong?"

At times, worry takes the shape of doubting whether or not God got it right, and as a result, doubt is the functional opposite of trust. Those doubts both derailed our ancient parents in the garden and debilitated the children of Israel in the wilderness. Likewise, doubts about God's goodness, wisdom, or purposes can severely impact our ability to walk by faith as we face the pressures and concerns of our own daily experiences.

Anxiety. Arguably the biblical poster child for anxiety is a surprising figure. After all, he was described as a man after God's own heart (1 Samuel 13:14), and in many ways and many times he lived up to that lofty descriptor. But the evidence of the Psalms seems to shout that David, Israel's hero and king, was a man who also struggled deeply with whether or not God would, in

Keller's words, "get it right," and many of his songs reflect that anxiety.

To dig into that a bit, the book of Psalms contains 150 songs and prayers and is divided into five books, and the first two books—the second of which ends with the line, "The prayers of David the son of Jesse are ended" (72:20)—are dominated by songs of lament, the bulk of them written by David. The man after God's heart clearly had a rough go of it in many ways.

In his younger years, David was hated and pursued by King Saul, becoming a vagabond with no home and, seemingly, no hope. Once he became king, David was driven from the throne by his own son Absalom and once again found himself without safety and under threat. David often responded to these and other life challenges by composing songs of lament.

Now to be fair, the troubles David experienced were very real things and should never be discounted. Nevertheless, the disproportionate number of lament psalms attributed to David should get our attention. It clearly makes a statement about David's heart and mind when his musical response to life was a dirge of lament rather than a hallelujah of faith (though those often came later).

When I was in seminary, I took a course, Exposition of Psalms, in which the prof, Ed Curtis, explained that the Psalms are fundamentally different from the rest of the Bible. He said that of the sixty-six books of the Bible, sixty-five of them are God speaking to us, while in the book of Psalms we speak to God. Yes, the Psalms are inspired by the Holy Spirit and are rightly included in Scripture.

But in the Psalms we get the gut-level, sometimes ugly, always honest human emotions of people engaged in the various seasons of life. At times these emotions produce moments of rapturous worship and celebration, while at other times they generate words of doubt, despair, anger, and, yes, anxiety.

David's anxiety regularly finds its lyric voice by asking how long it will be before God shows up and comes to his aid—if He ever does!

> And my soul is greatly horrified;
> But You, LORD—how long? (Psalm 6:3)

"Greatly horrified," sometimes translated "in deep anguish," is a powerful expression that describes the psalmist in such an emotional crisis that he cannot even comprehend what God might be doing in this season of trial. As a counterbalance to the children of Israel in the wilderness, it is as if David is wondering whether or not God will ever get it right.

In another of David's similar laments, we see the same cry of "how long" leading to a call for God's immediate rescue:

> Lord, how long will You look on?
> Rescue my soul from their ravages,
> My only life from the lions. (35:17)

Of Psalm 35:17, *The Expositor's Bible Commentary* underlines this core element of David's anxiety:

His enemies have become like wild animals. He laments to his God, "O Lord, how long will you look on?" The reference to God as "Lord" (=Master) may be deliberate. The Master of the universe must see all that the rogues have done, but how long will it be before he will act justly?

Will God get it right?

This theme carries on in many other lament psalms as well. While, according to its superscription, Psalm 42 is not a song of David, it conveys the same anxiety-filled concerns. Describing himself as a harried or perhaps even hunted deer, the singer thirsts for God (v. 1), longs for God's presence (v. 2), weeps continuously (v. 3), and grieves over lost opportunities for corporate worship (v. 4). In verse 5, it is as if the psalmist collects himself by prodding his own memory and reminds himself that his hope is in God.

But, as doubt is the functional opposite of trust, anxiety is the functional opposite of hope. No sooner has the psalmist buttressed his hope and confidence in God than the anxiety returns:

My soul is in despair within me. (v. 6)

This pattern repeats itself in verse 11 of Psalm 42 and then echoes forward into Psalm 43 with more reason for despair—which matters because many scholars see Psalm 43 as the third stanza of Psalm 42. Clearly if, as my seminary prof said, the Psalms are the expression of human emotion in the face of real-life experiences, then one of life's most consistent realities is anxiety over whether, or when, God will respond to our prayers and act on our behalf. Again, as the paraphrase of Tim Keller's words stated earlier, anxiety is fearing that God won't get it right.

Anxiety looks to the future with worry, while doubt, its near cousin, frets over the past. And the common thread between the two life responses is a gigantic question mark about the trustworthiness of God in the present.

What does such worry—whether it is looking back or looking forward—produce?

How Worry Hurts Us

When I was a boy, my dad lost his job because he would not compromise his integrity in areas that his bosses demanded him to. Jobless and with a gang of kids to feed, he pressed forward and started a job-placement agency specializing in executive, high-salaried, white-collar positions. Starting a business is not for the faint of heart. It is filled with stress factors that are only relieved by success.

Well, my dad was successful at placing people into these jobs but was less successful in getting them to pay the agreed-upon fee for the services he had provided for these now well-employed individuals. This meant that his income level had not improved and his debt had increased substantially, and he still had a passel of kids to feed.

I would see my dad come home from work and the pressure he was under was apparent—as were the worries that dogged him. It damaged his health, and the level of uncertainty in our household cast our family under a dark cloud of despair. The harder Dad worked, the deeper his fears and worries grew and the darker the atmosphere in our house became.

That is what worry does to us. It pushes us into dark places, both emotionally and spiritually. The wisdom of the Proverbs cautions us about the power of worry with these words:

> Worry weighs a person down;
>   an encouraging word cheers a person
>   up. (Proverbs 12:25 NLT)

While this proverb offers a reminder that encouragement can help the burdened person, the emphasis of the first half of the verse is what we need to see. "Worry weighs a person down." Worry creates burdens too heavy for us to bear, burdens we were never designed to be able to carry. I saw it in my dad, and I have seen it in the darker seasons of my own life (with my own passel of kids to feed).

In *Traveling Light*, Max Lucado describes the heavy burdens that worry creates this way:

> The burlap bag of worry. Cumbersome. Chunky. Unattractive. Scratchy. Hard to get a handle on. Irritating to carry and impossible to give away.

Everything about worry is tough. Everything about worry is challenging and difficult. Everything about worry weighs us down.

Poet Tony DeLorger describes *worry* as "self-imposed suffering," arguably the best definition of worry that I have ever heard or read. Worry hurts us because, by worrying, we isolate ourselves. We create a prison of our own making—and a prison from which escape is challenging indeed.

However, with all due respect to poet Tony DeLorger, I do think there is one way—and one way only—that worry can actually help us. Worry forces us to think.

How Worry Helps Us

By forcing us to think, worry can make us examine our belief systems. It can drive us to a level of self-examination that asks us whether we will believe our beliefs and doubt our doubts, or believe our doubts and doubt our beliefs.

In other words:

Will we believe that the problems we face are bigger than our God and His ability?

Will we allow our doubts and anxieties to define our view of life instead of the God we say has given us life?

Or . . .

Will we truly believe that God is who He claims to be?
Will we believe the Scriptures that we say and sing
    that we trust?

Worry, if responded to wisely, can force us into a moment of decision where we take stock of our convictions—and hopefully bring ourselves to the right course of action with our worries:

> Cast all your anxiety on Him, because He
> cares about you. (1 Peter 5:7)

But, What If . . . ?

Ultimately, worry is a battle of belief. And if worry can bring us to a willingness to trust God afresh, then even something as frustrating as worry can lead to a strengthening of our walk with our God. If we can learn in our seasons of worry to "cast all [our] anxiety on Him," then the lessons of life's darker experiences can actually encourage us in our faith. If not, then, as Tony DeLorger put it, "Worry is a burden without advantage."

However, hymn writer Edward Joy saw in worry an opportunity—an opportunity to understand our weakness and celebrate our God's strength. An opportunity to find rest and peace in the God who is greater than my needs and better than I sometimes think. Joy wrote:

> Is there a heart o'erbound by sorrow?
> Is there a life weighed down by care?

Come to the cross, each burden bearing;
All your anxiety—leave it there.

No other friend so swift to help you,
No other friend so quick to hear,
No other place to leave your burden,
No other one to hear your prayer.

All your anxiety, all your care,
Bring to the mercy seat, leave it there,
Never a burden He cannot bear,
Never a friend like Jesus!

This relationship of confident trust is the beautiful gift
we want to pursue together in these pages.

Questions for Personal Reflection or Group Discussion

1. My growing-up years conditioned me to worry during my first trip to Russia. Can you identify particular areas where your life experiences have created deeply engrained worry or fear?

2. We considered two different aspects of worry: doubts over events from the past and anxiety over situations that are yet future. Which do you find more difficult? Why?

3. How have you seen those doubts and anxieties affect your confidence in God? In His care? In His faithfulness?

4. What are some of the ways that specific areas of worry have created burdens you have tried to carry? How have you responded to those worries? Were those responses healthy or unhealthy?

5. Why can a healthy consideration of your level of trust in the Lord be a positive consequence of seasons of worry? How can that self-inventory prepare you for facing potential causes of worry that are yet to come?

Chapter Two

CAUSE AND EFFECT

If you believe that feeling bad or worrying long enough will change a past or future event, then you are residing on another planet with a different reality system.

—Wayne W. Dyer

It was a very bleak time to be an American. The pains and losses of the First World War had been glossed over by the excesses of the Roaring Twenties. Many historians believe that this era of extreme excess was a response to anxiety in almost every area of life in the United States as well as in much of the Western world. The Encyclopedia Britannica describes those anxieties:

> After the end of World War I, many Americans were left with a feeling of distrust toward foreigners and radicals, whom they held responsible for the war. The Russian

Revolution of 1917 and the founding of the communists' Third International in 1919 further fanned American fears of radicalism. Race riots and labour unrest added to the tension. Thus, when a series of strikes and indiscriminate bombings began in 1919, the unrelated incidents were all assumed—incorrectly in most cases—to be communist-inspired. During the ensuing Red Scare, civil liberties were sometimes grossly violated and many innocent aliens were deported. The Red Scare was over within a year, but a general distrust of foreigners, liberal reform movements, and organized labour remained throughout the 1920s. In fact, many viewed Warren G. Harding's landslide victory in 1920 as a repudiation of Woodrow Wilson's internationalism and of the reforms of the Progressive era.

This season of prosperity was quickly undone. On October 28, 1929—sometimes remembered as Black Monday—the stock market began to crash, plunging the United States and much of the world into what would become the Great Depression. This season of economic crisis extended for almost four years, with the world experiencing at one point a 24 percent unemployment rate and a decline in the gross domestic product of almost 27 percent. It seemed that the only establishments doing a brisk business were the soup kitchens and the breadlines.

In November of 1932, Franklin Delano Roosevelt was elected as the thirty-second president of the United States—with the national morale joining the economy at an all-time low. That was the context for Roosevelt's first inauguration. On March 4, 1933, in his inaugural address, Roosevelt opened with what would become some of the most famous words he ever spoke as president:

> I am certain that my fellow Americans expect that on my induction into the Presidency I will address them with a candor and a decision which the present situation of our Nation impels. This is preeminently the time to speak the truth, the whole truth, frankly and boldly. Nor need we shrink from honestly facing conditions in our country today. This great Nation will endure as it has endured, will revive and will prosper. So, first of all, let me assert my firm belief that the only thing we have to fear is fear itself—nameless, unreasoning, unjustified terror which paralyzes needed efforts to convert retreat into advance.

"The only thing we have to fear is fear itself." This was a bold and almost belligerent statement of challenge. Yet, while clearly inspirational, was it actually true? Was there nothing to fear but fear itself? For the person with a family to feed, it would seem that there was a lot to fear. For the families crowded together in a relative's house because they had lost their homes, it would seem that there was a lot to fear. For the unemployed workers living in shanties—communities called Hoovervilles as a protest against Roosevelt's predecessor, Herbert Hoover—it would seem that there was a lot to fear.

In the ensuing years since Roosevelt's words, there have been wars and anti-war protests, economic highs and lows, battles over civil rights and injustice, social upheaval, and global pandemics. And that's just the so-called big stuff. That doesn't even include a million different things that we fear on a personal level. With all due respect to President Roosevelt, it would seem that we still have a lot more to fear than fear itself.

Now, you may be wondering, Why are we spending all of this time talking about fear? Isn't this a book about worry? Yes, it is—but while psychologists draw a very clear line of differentiation between fear and worry, the two are very much related. And I would suggest to you that, when carefully considered, all worry finds its ultimate roots in fear.

Fear as Distinct from Worry

Gavin de Becker, in his book *The Gift of Fear*, offers a helpful analysis of the differences between fear and worry. He writes:

Real fear is a signal intended to be very brief, a mere servant of intuition. But though few would argue that extended, unanswered fear is destructive, millions choose to stay there. They may have forgotten or never learned that fear is not an emotion like sadness or happiness, either of which might last a long while. It is not a state, like anxiety. True fear is a survival signal that sounds only in the presence of danger, yet unwarranted fear has assumed a power over us that it holds over no other creature on earth.

Clearly this is why de Becker chose to entitle his book *The Gift of Fear*. Fear is not a one-size-fits-all emotion. While it can be destructive, it can also be lifesaving. Having a healthy fear of God is the most obvious positive aspect of fear at its best. Proverbs 9:10 tells us:

> The fear of the LORD is the beginning of
>   wisdom,
> And the knowledge of the Holy One is
>   understanding.

This type of fear, when dealing with human authority, expresses itself through respect and keeping the law, as Paul told the church at Rome:

> Render therefore to all their due: taxes to
> whom taxes are due, customs to whom

customs, fear to whom fear, honor to whom honor. (Romans 13:7 NKJV)

Not all fear is created equal. For instance, while the word *fear* is used in both of these cases, the meaning is different from our normal concept of fear. Our common understanding of fear has more to do with terror, while the fear of the Lord speaks more to awe or reverence. In relation to human authority the impact of fear is to elicit respect and honor. To see the positive aspects of frightened fear or afraid fear, we need to dig a little bit deeper.

Remember de Becker's comment that fear is "a survival signal that sounds only in the presence of danger." At its best, fear warns us so that we can prepare to face some oncoming danger. This fear may be induced by danger that confronts us or danger that confronts those we care about.

In what was voted on CMT (Country Music Television) as the eighth-best country music song of all time, Glen Campbell and Jimmy Webb combined to produce the haunting and beautiful song "Galveston." Written and released at the height of the Vietnam War, Campbell's glorious tenor voice gave soul and emotion to Webb's brilliant lyrics to give us a glimpse into the heart of a soldier at war who is longing for home.

This singing soldier thinks of his home on the waters of the Gulf of Mexico. The beaches. The waves. His girlfriend. Especially his girlfriend. And he thinks of all those things as cannons roar and he prepares to go into battle again. His overwhelming emotion?

I am so afraid of dying.

I did not go to Vietnam, spared that test by a high draft number when I turned eighteen (although I will confess that I was certainly worried about what my number would be!). But many of my friends *did* experience the war in Vietnam and expressed that same fear—that any moment might be their last and that all they had left behind, including the loves of their lives, would be lost to them forever. I am convinced that the reason "Galveston" endured and continues today to have a poignancy that is unusual in popular music is because that elemental sense of fear is so real. And while our fears may not include battlefield trauma, they have similar characteristics that can create anxiety and worry.

This is true in the spiritual realm as well. The apostle Paul wrote to people he cared about in the church at Thessalonica, saying:

> For this reason, when I could no longer endure it, I also sent to find out about your faith, for fear that the tempter might have tempted you, and our labor would be for nothing. (1 Thessalonians 3:5)

Paul's friends appear to be in a place where they are facing active opposition from their spiritual enemy—Satan. And Paul is fearful (here the word *fear* speaks of a desperate concern) on their behalf, knowing the damage that could be done to them if their foe lured them away from the life of faith in Christ. This very real danger caused legitimate fear that drove Paul to respond with concern for their well-being.

The same positive fear that caused Glen Campbell's soldier to recognize the dangers of battle and caused Paul to be concerned for his Thessalonian brothers and sisters in Christ is the positive fear that causes us to question the wisdom of dangerous situations.

> Having fallen off a bridge, I can tell you that I approach heights with a genuine sense of caution.
>
> Having been in several automobile crashes in my life, I have learned the value of driving defensively.
>
> Having lost my father to heart failure, I recognize the need for maintaining good heart health.

You can list your own experiences that have taught you to fear wisely. The key here is that all of those cautions are driven by a healthy fear of circumstances that life can throw our way—and that demand a response that, to the best of our ability, minimizes the danger.

But that is healthy fear. Fear that responds with appropriate action and wisdom. The unhealthy response to fear is worry.

Fear as Worry's Main Trigger

If we return to Gavin de Becker's analysis in *The Gift of Fear*, he describes worry as a choice, a destructive way of responding to the things that make us afraid:

> *Worry is the fear we manufacture*—it is not authentic. If you choose to worry about

40

something, have at it, but do so knowing
it's a choice. . . . After decades of seeing
worry in all its forms, I've concluded that
it hurts people much more than it helps. It
interrupts clear thinking, wastes time, and
shortens life.

Perhaps the two biblical poster children for this level
of fear-induced anxiety were, ironically, both kings. As
William Shakespeare rightly put it in *Henry IV, Part 2*,
"Uneasy lies the head that wears a crown." A person who
carries great responsibility or enjoys a position of great
authority and power has an entirely different set of fears
that trigger worry and anxiety in their minds.

In 1 Samuel 9, Saul was declared Israel's first king. The
crowning of Saul would prove to be a massive mistake
for two significant reasons. First, the Israelites' request
for a king was motivated by the wrong reasons. Rather
than choosing to continue as a theocracy (a monarchy in
which God himself was the king), their desire was to be
like "all the nations" (8:5). Rejecting their unique status
as the chosen people of God, Israel chose to model themselves after the pagan cultures that surrounded them.

Second, the criteria for that king was also tragically
misguided—and is captured in the description of Saul in
1 Samuel 9:2:

[Kish] had a son whose name was Saul, a
young and handsome man, and there was
not a more handsome man than he among

the sons of Israel; from his shoulders and
up he was taller than any of the people.

A leader who looks good is not necessarily the same thing as a leader who leads well. That sad truth was proven as Saul moved from early victories to continued failures, causing God to remove the throne from him and give it to young David. The result? Uneasy rest for King Saul who, though having enlisted David as an ally after his battle with Goliath, lived in constant fear of losing his crown. This fear produced an anxiety so intense that it took on a kind of mental illness—and drove Saul to a murderous pursuit of David to remove this threat to his position and power.

Years later, another king, Herod the Great, was a man whose rest was likewise uneasy. A brilliant builder and engineer, Herod—who was Idumaean, not Jewish—was also a ruthless ruler who would do anything to protect his grip upon Israel's throne as a vassal king of Rome. So fierce were his anxieties about lost power that he had a number of family members, including his wife Mariamne I, executed to remove any threat to his reign.

It is no surprise, then, that Herod responded with violence to the fear of losing his throne to David's greater son, Jesus. When magi from the east came seeking the newborn Jewish king, they arrived at the seat of power in Jerusalem (see Matthew 2:1–12). Upon hearing of a child-king who had been born in Bethlehem, Herod's response—like Saul's before him—was a fear-induced anxiety that sought blood. Desperate to hold on to his crown,

Herod ordered the murder of all male infants in Bethlehem under the age of two.

As Saul's and Herod's stories remind us, the more one has, the more one has to lose—and as a result, the more one has to worry about. That is why crowned heads aren't the only ones that rest uneasily. And loss of power and position are not the only fears that can trigger worry or anxiety.

The Fears That Trigger Our Worries

The Merriam-Webster online dictionary says that, in science, a *catalyst* is "a substance that enables a chemical reaction to proceed at a usually faster rate or under different conditions (as at a lower temperature) than otherwise possible." In life, a *catalyst* is "an agent that provokes or speeds significant change or action." In our discussion of worry, the fears that we respond to wrongly become the catalysts that can provoke worry or anxiety within us.

In chapter 1 we saw that, while there are many forms of worry, they essentially coalesce into two distinct categories—anxieties about the future and doubts about the past. Similarly, while there are many specific causes for worry, it seems to me that they all land in three particular categories—the unknown, the uncontrollable, and the nature of our fallen world. These become the catalysts—or triggers—that can take fears into unhealthy places, rob us of peace, and create within us stresses that can be destructive.

The unknown. It has often been said, "What you don't

know can't hurt you." I could not disagree more strongly. What we don't know can hurt us—and it can especially hurt us internally with stress. In J. R. R. Tolkien's *The Lord of the Rings*, Frodo Baggins and his friends (the Fellowship of the Ring) set out to return the One Ring to Mordor where it can be destroyed. For Frodo and his three Hobbit friends in particular, every step of the journey from their home in the Shire to Mordor is marked by anxiety because these little Hobbits know virtually nothing of life outside the Shire. They are the inexperienced, the unaware, the unsophisticated who have no actual idea of what lies ahead. It is a formula for fear—and a source for worry.

In a less dramatic but just as real way, every single person faces similar experiential crossroads that are blanketed by the unknown. The brave new world that is ensconced in the first day of school (at almost any level) can be terrifying. That first step into a new classroom or lunchroom or playground is filled with unknowns that are anxiety builders of the first order. The same applies to your first day at a new job, or the first day of a new marriage, or the first day with a new baby. The knowns are so overwhelmingly outweighed by the unknowns that the situation— even the most wonderful and blessed of situations—can begin to feel suffocating.

I was twenty-one years old when I went away to Bible college. I had worked in the secular business world and traveled for work, spending much time away from home. I was in no way uninitiated in life—but I was dreadfully uninitiated in *this*. I remember the bleakness of the moment as my mom and dad pulled out of the school's parking lot in the family station wagon and drove away. And I remember a sense of near panic at what lay ahead as the tailgate drifted into the distance. I had no friends there. I had come to the school to find a wife and play football (not necessarily in that order) and was now drowning in a sea of emotional turmoil. I knew a lot about life, but I knew nothing about what the next five minutes, five days, or five weeks might produce.

Fear of the unknown can be crippling. And when it is, it can trigger within us worries and anxieties that darken our hearts and cloud our minds.

The uncontrollable. Former New York Yankees baseball player Mickey Rivers said, "I don't get upset over things I can control, because if I can control them there's no sense in getting upset. And I don't get upset over things I can't control, because if I can't control them there's no sense in getting upset."

While that is a worthy goal and a noble thought—and actually true—I have to confess that, at least for me, it is much easier said than done. I'm not sure that anything scares us more than the things we can't control—which at some level is almost everything.

In the poem "Invictus," William Ernest Henley, a self-proclaimed atheist, wrote:

> I am the master of my fate,
> I am the captain of my soul.

But was he really? Henley suffered from a variety of diseases, including tuberculosis, and no amount of positive thinking or self-determination could overcome those challenges. Master of his fate? Captain of his soul? Not likely. No matter how we might wish that to be so, there are more uncontrollable elements to life than we can count.

That is where we all live. We can't control our children. We can't control the economy. We can't control our job security. We can't control our health. We can't control our relationships. We can't control the arrival of catastrophic weather events. We can't control . . . We can't control . . . We can't control.

One of the great worry-inducing fear factors of life is the reality that, no matter how we might wish it weren't so, there are few things in life over which we have absolute control.

A broken and evil world. This may be the most challenging of these triggers for worry because it is so beyond us. Our world has been broken by sin, and people have been broken with it. This is at the root of one of the great theological and philosophical concerns debated in the halls of higher education—the problem of evil in the world.

How do you prepare yourself to live in a world where something like the Holocaust can take place? How do you process the real dangers of living in a world where schools in Columbine, Newtown, and Uvalde are the literal targets of mass murderers? How do you understand a world where racial injustice exists on a global scale? How do you respond to horrifying events of genocide, whether based on national differences, religious disagreement, or ethnic disparity?

For those who deny the presence of evil in the world,

there are no meaningful explanations. Our world is broken by sin and, as such, is a world afflicted with evil. And that can be absolutely terrifying.

Fear of the unknown. Fear of the uncontrollable. Fear of evil in the world.

These catalysts for anxiety are real; they are not imaginary. And the longer one lives, the more one realizes how genuinely threatening these elements of creation's brokenness really are. Yes, it certainly seems that we have plenty to be afraid of in this fragile life we live.

Nothing to Fear

We began this chapter by considering FDR's inspirational assertion that we have nothing to fear but fear itself. Unfortunately, fear itself is the seedbed for many of the worries that dog our days. Whether those fears are rooted in life's unpredictability, our lack of control over the circumstances of life, or the world's brokenness, fear cannot be ignored.

Life's fears must be faced, and when we do face them, thankfully we have in our God the greatest of all resources for addressing the worry-inducing fears we experience. As David, in one of his better moments, wrote in Psalm 34:4:

> I sought the LORD and He answered me,
> And rescued me from all my fears.

But how do we do this? Perhaps one place to start is in

remembering that the walk of faith is, in fact, a walk of *faith*. We make our way through this troubled world in a trust relationship with our Creator. We learn to trust Him by trusting Him—and that experience becomes a platform for trusting God in deeper, even more fearful moments of anxiety. In a sense, our ability to rest in God is strengthened by our past experiences of His faithfulness and trustworthiness.

Again, David provides a useful example. We know from reading his many lament psalms that he often struggled with trusting God (like we often do as well). But in his best moments, he could look back on episodes of God's faithfulness to stir his confidence in the present crisis. For instance, when preparing to face off against Goliath, David cited times when God enabled him to defeat both a bear and a lion who threatened his father's flocks (1 Samuel 17:34–37). It was in his past experiences with his God that David found the ability to trust God in the present crisis. As we likewise walk by faith, we too can build a reservoir of such experiences with God—and allow His past faithfulness to inform how we respond to present challenges.

Ultimately, this was the confidence addressed by Martin Luther in his classic hymn "A Mighty Fortress Is Our God" (in German "Ein Feste Burg"). Luther approached the problems, dangers, and, yes, fears that come along with life in a fallen world by reminding us that our God is greater than the fears that germinate into worries. He wrote:

> And though this world, with devils filled,
> Should threaten to undo us,

We will not fear, for God has willed
His truth to triumph through us.
The prince of darkness grim,
We tremble not for him;
His rage we can endure,
For lo! his doom is sure;
One little word shall fell him.

Luther's majestic hymn was inspired by Psalm 46, and it offers us tangible reminders of the real and true solution to our fears—the God who is our mighty fortress.

Questions for Personal Reflection or Group Discussion

1. Are you a fearful person? Consider an experience when you have known significant fear. What was at its root? What was your response? What were the results?

2. What is the difference between healthy and unhealthy fear? What is an example of each? Which kind of fear do you more commonly experience—healthy or unhealthy?

3. How are the fears and anxieties of King Saul and King Herod similar to your own? How are they different? How can their stories be cautionary tales to you regarding how you respond to your own fears and anxieties?

4. We considered three areas of fear that are serious triggers for worry or anxiety. Which do you struggle with the most—the unknown, the uncontrollable, or the state of the world? Give an example, and both a healthy and an unhealthy response.

5. The kinds of fears we have considered in this chapter have the capacity to be overwhelming. Spend a few moments reflecting on Psalm 34:4 and why our Shepherd enables us to not need to fear.

Chapter Three

PROFESSIONAL WORRYING: BIBLE STYLE

There is only one way to happiness and that is to cease worrying about things which are beyond the power of our will.

—Epictetus

Heroes are heroes for a reason. At first glance, they appear almost flawless, providing a faultless role model that always gets it right and never gets it wrong. As a boy, I felt exactly that way about Davy Crockett, the king of the wild frontier. As such, I have spent much of my life reading everything I can get my hands on about the life of this hero of the Battle of the Alamo.

Yet, while in no way denting the heroism Crockett displayed in many seasons of his life, as I grew up I began to develop a grown-up understanding of my hero. He faced problems and heartaches and failures and struggles—repeated financial reversals, the death of his wife, and a failed political career to name just a few. Yes, he was a truly great man in a time in history when great men made great marks on their world, but he was also a flawed and sometimes troubled human being. In understanding some of the struggles that dogged his days, my grown-up version of Crockett actually allowed me to respect and admire him even *more*—because in order to be heroic, he had to overcome the life struggles that feel so familiar to those of us who aren't heroes in the historic sense of the word.

This pondering of my childhood hero has been a helpful exercise, because it has informed my understanding of the heroes of the Scriptures. The same people who in one moment were giants of the faith could in another moment buckle under the pressure and weight of the anxieties of life. For those of us who grew up watching Bible cartoons or hearing Bible stories told via flannelgraph in Sunday school, this is an important corrective. It is not disrespectful to acknowledge the simple reality that the biblical heroes we heard of as children were flawed human beings like the rest of us. The only perfect life was that of Jesus himself. All of the other people mentioned in the Bible were made of the same broken clay as we are.

My point is this: When we are overwhelmed with anxiety and drawn into seasons of worry, we are not on an untraveled trail. The great characters of the Scriptures, while usually noted for their faith-filled exploits, lived in the same world as we do. They faced the same concerns and struggles as we do. They too were given to anxiety.

We saw in the previous chapter that fear and worry are interrelated—and that fear triggers the anxieties that can weigh us down. These are the same catalysts for anxiety faced by heroes of the Bible, and while the word *worry* may not appear in the telling of their stories, their fear-driven anxieties are readily apparent. Let's consider some of them together.

Abraham

It is remarkable to ponder the massive steps of faith that were necessary in order for Abraham to leave his home and family and travel to a land unknown—simply because it was what God told him to do. From what we are given in the Scriptures, it appears that he'd had no previous exposure to the creator God, yet it seems that he instantly answered God's call. The writer of the letter to the Hebrews described Abraham's deep faith this way:

> By faith Abraham, when he was called, obeyed by going out to a place which he was to receive for an inheritance; and he left, not knowing where he was going. By faith he lived as a stranger in the land of promise, as in a foreign land, living in tents. (11:8–9)

The very imagery of such a move is captured by dramatic descriptors like "not knowing," "stranger," "foreign," and "living in tents." Leaving an established home and venturing into the unknown would have required faith and substantial courage.

Earlier we considered together the overwhelming pressures created by the fear of the unknown, and I would suggest to you that Abraham faced this great fear and ventured into the unknown with nothing to hang on to but God's promises. Little wonder, then, that Abraham is considered the father of the faithful and a hero of faith, and rightly so.

But, like Crockett, Abraham had blind spots. Abraham had pressure points. And one of his most profound pressure points was his beautiful wife, Sarah. In 1979, recording artists Dr. Hook & the Medicine Show released a semi-campy song that spoke of the fears and dangers produced "When You're in Love with a Beautiful Woman." Abraham lived those fears personally—and the resulting anxieties produced choices that were decidedly counter to the heart of faith that so often had characterized Abraham's experience.

> Now there was a famine in the land; so Abram went down to Egypt to live there for a time, because the famine was severe in the land. It came about, when he was approaching Egypt, that he said to his wife Sarai, "See now, I know that you are a beautiful woman; and when the Egyptians see you, they will say, 'This is his wife'; and they will kill me, but they will let you live. Please say that you are my sister so that it

may go well for me because of you, and that I may live on account of you." (Genesis 12:10–13)

This happened not only once but twice. In Genesis 20, Abraham and his family had traveled to the Negev, into an area known as Gerar which was ruled by Abimelech. Once again, Abraham asked Sarah to lie about the true nature of their relationship out of fear that he might be killed in order that the king could take her as his own. Setting aside for a moment that at this point Sarah was some ninety years old yet still considered so beautiful that men would kill for her, the focus rests solidly on Abraham—and his fear-based anxiety. And it is likewise fascinating to me that Abraham's son Isaac responded to this very fear-based anxiety in exactly the same way years later when he and his wife visited Gerar. As the popular adage goes, "History doesn't repeat itself, but it often rhymes."

It seems truly amazing that this man of faith who left hearth and home to journey into an unknown land among unknown peoples to experience an unknown future would crumble under a different set of pressures. It is clear that his primary concern was not for Sarah and her welfare—but for himself. It also seems clear that, while he had previously trusted God to provide for him and protect him on his unprecedented pilgrimage to Canaan, he was unwilling or perhaps unable to trust God with the dangers in both Egypt and Gerar that were possible but by no means certain.

Abraham was a hero of faith—filled with anxiety over fears that were imagined.

Jacob

If I may be allowed a moment of absolute candor, though one of the patriarchs of the Jewish people and an heir to God's promise to bless all nations, Jacob is one of my least favorite characters in the Bible. His name itself means "heel grabber" and speaks of one who tries to take an advantage over others, one who seeks to trip up others for personal gain—and nowhere was that truer than in his relationship with his brother, Esau.

As one who has three brothers, I have full understanding of how hard it is to be brothers. Competition is the currency of brotherly relationships, and when that competition is healthy it can be a motivator toward significant accomplishment. Before my brother David passed away, three of us brothers and one of our brothers-in-law would periodically get together for a weekend of golf. But it was more than golf. It was a kind of full-contact golf that involved constant ribbing, nonstop needling, and pressure being applied at every shot. It was brutal—and just about the most fun that you can have. Why? Because behind all the needling and sly remarks was a genuine love and respect that we had for one another. That is competition at its best. It is competition that is healthy.

When competition is unhealthy, however, it can be heartbreaking at best and murderous at worst. Which brings us back to Jacob and Esau—early prototypes of sibling rivalry. The older twin, Esau found favor in the eyes of their father, Isaac, while Jacob was preferred by their mother, Rebekah. This competition would find its ultimate climax in a battle of sorts over two cultural factors that were held in inestimable value—the birthright and the blessing.

In ancient cultures, the birthright was the right of inheritance and leadership of the family that fell to the firstborn son. The blessing was a statement of honor that affirmed that the firstborn would receive the position and status secured in the birthright. In one of the Bible's more familiar stories, Jacob, the heel grabber, tripped up his brother, Esau, by bartering a bowl of stew for the birthright (Genesis 25), then stole the blessing outright by deceiving their father—aided and abetted by Rebekah, his mom (Genesis 27).

This obviously unhealthy competition for the position and status of the favored son resulted in a murderous rage in Esau—a rage that prompted Jacob to flee to the country of his ancestors, where he lived for more than twenty years. There, Jacob himself was tripped up by another relative, his uncle Laban, but he eventually began the long journey back to Canaan with a large family and vast possessions of livestock (Genesis 29–31).

Yet if it appears that Jacob was returning home the conquering hero, he felt no confidence in that return. Why? Jacob had some rather substantial unfinished business with the brother he had cheated years before. To try to forestall disaster, Jacob sent messengers to Esau to announce his return. The response he received from the messengers was not encouraging:

> The messengers returned to Jacob, saying, "We came to your brother Esau, and

furthermore he is coming to meet you, and four hundred men are with him." Then Jacob was greatly afraid and distressed. (32:6–7)

There it is. Fear-induced distress, and understandably so. *The Expositor's Bible Commentary* says:

> Much suspense surrounds Jacob's reunion with his brother, Esau. Like Jacob himself, we the readers are kept in the dark about Esau's intentions. Why is he coming with four hundred (v. 6) men to meet Jacob on his return? When last we heard about Esau, his intention was to take revenge on Jacob for his stolen blessing (27:41). Jacob's fear that Esau may now come to do just that seems well founded.

Yet as we have seen, while fear is often very real, it is in those moments of stress and pressure that our truest selves are most clearly revealed. Jacob's response to this distress? To attempt to bribe Esau into receiving him without revenge. In a sense, as he bought Esau's birthright with a bowl of stew, Jacob now seeks to buy Esau's acceptance with gifts of livestock and wealth.

> And [Esau] said, "What do you mean by all this company which I have met?" And he said, "To find favor in the sight of my

lord." But Esau said, "I have plenty, my brother; let what you have be your own." Jacob said, "No, please, if now I have found favor in your sight, then accept my gift from my hand, for I see your face as one sees the face of God, and you have received me favorably. Please accept my gift which has been brought to you, because God has dealt graciously with me and because I have plenty." (33:8–11)

Interestingly, while Abraham's anxiety caused him to go against his dominant characteristic—faith—Jacob's fear-fed worries caused him to revert to form. A schemer and conniver once again sought to protect himself by scheming and conniving. While Abraham's sudden lack of faith was a surprise, Jacob's pattern of heel grabbing for his own personal advantage is, sadly, no surprise whatsoever.

Gideon

A ministry that I have long held in high regard is the ministry of The Gideons International. A collective of Christian businessmen and businesswomen, their ministry is one of Bible distribution. Whether at schools, hospitals, military installations, or, famously, hotels, Gideon Bibles are readily available to anyone with spiritual needs or questions. Beginning in Wisconsin in 1899, the founders of Gideons wrestled with what to name this new organization. Their website says:

When it came time to decide the name of the Association, the men held a special prayer time to ask that God might lead them to select the proper name. After, Mr. Knights arose from his knees and said simply, "We shall be called Gideons." He then proceeded to read the story of Gideon from the sixth and seventh chapters of Judges.

At first blush, this does not seem like a match. The story of Gideon certainly is a fascinating one, but it focuses on combat as opposed to the advancement of the Scriptures (which at that time would have been the Torah—the five books of Moses). Yet every copy of the Scriptures printed by the Gideons has emblazoned on the cover a jar with a flame issuing from it, which directly links the Gideons to the story of Gideon. To see why, we should join Mr. Knights in Judges 6.

The era of the judges was a mixed bag of experiences in Israel. What some scholars call the "cycle of apostasy" meant that Israel's chronic disobedience and dalliances with idolatry would result in God's discipline, and then His provision of a judge—a leader and rescuer—would bring them rescue and restoration to their God. This rescue would then, eventually, be followed by another lapse into idolatry. And so on. And so on. Over and over again.

Gideon was one of those judges and entered the story as Israel was feeling the pressure of Midian—the instrument of God's chastening in this particular season of correction. The angel of the Lord called Gideon to service with a powerful assurance:

> The LORD is with you, valiant warrior. (Judges 6:12)

This promise resonates with the heart of every child of God. Jesus came as Immanuel, which means "God with us" (Matthew 1:23). The resurrected Master also affirmed His ever-abiding presence with us in the Great Commission, saying, "I am with you always" (28:20). As we will see in a later chapter, Hebrews 13:5 echoes Deuteronomy 31:6, reminding us that our God "will not desert you or abandon you."

The assurance of God's presence didn't answer all of Gideon's questions, but it did get him moving. Yet in Judges 6 it is clear that he is anxious about the coming battle with the Midianites. How is it clear? By the almost desperate need for a guarantee of the coming battle's outcome. That desperation seems evident in Gideon's prayers:

> Then Gideon said to God, "If You are going to save Israel through me, as You have spoken, behold, I am putting a fleece of wool on the threshing floor. If there is dew on the fleece only, and it is dry on all the ground, then I will know that You will save Israel through me, as You have spoken." And it was so. When he got up

early the next morning and wrung out the fleece, he wrung the dew from the fleece, a bowl full of water. Then Gideon said to God, "Do not let Your anger burn against me, so that I may speak only one more time; please let me put you to the test only one more time with the fleece: let it now be dry only on the fleece, and let there be dew on all the ground." And God did so that night; for it was dry only on the fleece, and dew was on all the ground. (vv. 36–40)

For those of us who grew up hearing about "fleece praying," this was the moment when Gideon invented it. Fleece praying can be defined as demanding a sign by God to provide advance information of future outcomes. I certainly relate to Gideon's desire for guarantees, but I also recognize that a guarantee precludes the need for trust. This takes us back to what we saw in chapter 1—sometimes worry is the anxiety that God won't get it right. The need for a guarantee exposes that anxiety, and Gideon's prayers for fleeces both wet and dry underscore why living by faith is so hard. Living by faith has no guarantees—except the one that matters most.

God will never leave or forsake us.

The angelic call which assured God's presence with Gideon was actually far more significant than any amount of fleece prayers or tests. Why? Because the only reason that Gideon could ever be a "valiant warrior" (Judges

6:12) was because the Lord *was* with him. Whereas Abraham, the man of faith, struggled with doubts, and Jacob, the heel grabber, tended toward manipulation and scheming, Gideon was different. It appears that he struggled to believe that he could really trust the promise of God's unfailing presence.

And, like Gideon, sometimes we do as well.

Moses

In one of the first books I read as a young Christ follower, *Failure: The Back Door to Success*, pastor and teacher Erwin Lutzer provides a fresh perspective for some of life's most difficult moments. To say the least, the concept is rather bittersweet. No matter what endeavor we start out upon, we want to succeed. No one ever began a new job or a new marriage or a new experience by saying, "Wow, I really hope that I fail big-time here." We all want to succeed, and more to the point here, we all want to succeed *always*. If I am honest, there have been times when, had I known that the path to success wound through a season of failure, I would have been sorely tempted to opt out. Success feels good. Failure hurts. Success fosters admiration. Failure often produces embarrassment—even humiliation.

This brings us to Moses. Moses would become arguably one of the greatest leaders of all time, leading the children of Israel out of bondage in Egypt, into their establishment as a covenant people of God, through the forty years of wilderness wanderings, and to the very threshold of the land promised to the people of Israel by God so many years before. By any definition, that is a remarkable career as a leader. But Moses was eighty years into his life before he experienced his greatest achievements. Earlier in life, a moment of failure drove him into the wilderness where his previous brashness was replaced by insecure uncertainty.

You probably know the story. Israel was enslaved in Egypt and the male children were being exterminated, but Moses was rescued by the bravery of his mother, the clever thinking of his sister, and the compassion of Pharaoh's daughter (Exodus 2:1–10). Being raised in the king's palace, Moses had the privileges of education, acclaim, and military success (Acts 7:22)—privileges unheard of for the son of slaves. But when he saw a Hebrew being mistreated by one of the taskmasters, Moses stepped in, took justice into his own hands, and killed the Egyptian. Stephen in his historic homily in Acts 7 makes it clear that Moses assumed he was to lead Israel out of slavery (v. 25)—and apparently he attempted to do that by his own strength. Why not? He had enjoyed much success as a leader and must have expected to see that success roll on.

Instead, he became persona non grata and was driven from Egypt into the mountains of Midian. Fast-forward forty years, and the now eighty-year-old shepherd has little to commend him. In fact, his once unshakable confidence seems almost beyond repair. So in Exodus 3, when God comes to him in a bush that burns without burning up, we discover a Moses who is almost the polar opposite of what his younger self had been. Brashness has been replaced with insecurity. Confidence has been replaced by fear. Initiative has been replaced by anxiety.

At this point in his life, it is unlikely that Moses considered his earlier failure as a prelude to success. Far from it. Listen to his protests as he responds to God's call:

> Who am I, that I should go to Pharaoh, and that I should bring the sons of Israel out of Egypt? (3:11)

> What if they will not believe me or listen to what I say? For they may say, "The LORD has not appeared to you." (4:1)

> Please, Lord, I have never been eloquent, neither recently nor in time past, nor since You have spoken to Your servant; for I am slow of speech and slow of tongue. (4:10)

Three attempts to escape God's call that I am convinced found their roots in his failure forty years earlier. Once the prince of Egypt, Moses now is afraid to face the king. Once a man in command, he now is afraid of rejection. Once an eloquent speaker (Acts 7:22), Moses now feels inadequate to speak. Where Abraham feared death, Jacob worried about revenge, and Gideon was anxious about the unknowns, Moses is worried about failing—again. He knows the bitter taste of failure and does not see that failure as the path to success. He sees that failure as a platform for still more failure.

Moses's anxiety in the presence of the Almighty shows that he saw this call not as an opportunity to fulfill a mission he had claimed decades earlier but as a possibility for disaster that must be avoided.

Yes, God would prevail and Israel would be liberated and Moses would become one of the greatest heroes of the Old Testament. But on that Midian hillside, all of that seemed very far away, shrouded under a dark cloud of anxiety that was fostered by the misgivings that only come from experiences of great failure.

Calling All Heroes

We began by talking about heroes, and this chapter has been filled with them. But human heroes. Flawed heroes. Broken heroes. This is important because it was not my intent to in any way diminish the greatness of these Jewish heroes of the Old Testament. Far from it. It was my intent that we see the genuine humanity of these heroes which demanded that they live in reliance upon God. When they did, God used them as His instruments to accomplish amazing things.

I think of Billy Graham, a young man from North Carolina whose relatively simple background might not seem like adequate preparation for a world-shaking ministry of evangelism. Or Mother Teresa and the impact she had on countless lives among India's poorest and most vulnerable. Or Dr. M. R. DeHaan, who overcame the fear of joblessness and, upon counsel from a good friend, founded a small radio ministry that grew into a global enterprise for the gospel.

When the heroes of the Bible allowed their reliance on God to be replaced with anxiety over the unknowns, uncontrollables, or brokennesses of this world, this life that was already challenging became suffocating. Just like it does for us. These Old Testament heroes are not heroes because they always got it right and never failed. They are heroes because they found in God what they could never find in themselves.

Just like us.

Hebrews 11 records these individuals as heroes of the Old Testament because, for all of their shortcomings, they learned the lessons of walking "by faith."

> *Abraham:* "*By faith* Abraham, when he was called, obeyed by going out to a place which he was to receive for an inheritance; and he left, not knowing where he was going." (v. 8)

> *Jacob:* "*By faith* Jacob, as he was dying, blessed each of the sons of Joseph, and worshiped, leaning on the top of his staff." (v. 21)

> *Moses:* "*By faith* Moses, when he had grown up, refused to be called the son of Pharaoh's daughter, choosing rather to endure ill-treatment with the people of God than to enjoy the temporary plea-sures of sin, considering the reproach of Christ greater riches than the treasures of Egypt; for he was looking to the reward. *By faith* he left Egypt,

not fearing the wrath of the king; for he persevered, as though seeing Him who is unseen. *By faith* he kept the Passover and the sprinkling of the blood, so that the destroyer of the firstborn would not touch them." (vv. 24–28)

Gideon: "And what more shall I say? For time will fail me if I tell of Gideon. . . ." (v. 32; all emphases added)

It is in God's presence, care, and provision that we endure. And it is in Him that our anxiety and worry are replaced with the peace that passes understanding (Philippians 4:6–7). That was the reassuring truth that Catharina von Schlegel was embracing in her own heart—and leading us to embrace in ours—when in 1752 she wrote the words of one of the church's most enduring hymns:

> Be still, my soul: the Lord is on thy side.
> Bear patiently the cross of grief or pain.
> Leave to thy God to order and provide;
> In every change, He faithful will remain.
> Be still, my soul: thy best, thy heav'nly
>   Friend
> Through thorny ways leads to a joyful end.

As with the Old Testament heroes of the faith we've seen, our ultimate hope and help in times of struggle and fear is found in the God whose love for us never fails. Our worries should never be allowed to displace our trust in and reliance upon that love.

Questions for Personal Reflection or Group Discussion

1. Who were your childhood heroes? What attracted you to them? In what ways were you inspired by them? In what ways did you try to emulate them?

2. Abraham's faith was tested when he imagined that his life was threatened. What faith-stretching moments have you experienced? In the end, were the threats real or imagined?

3. Jacob worried about the revenge that he felt Esau would bring against him. Have you ever hurt someone to the point where revenge felt like a possibility? How did you respond to that possibility?

4. Gideon faced the future demanding guaranteed outcomes. Why is that desire for guarantees unrealistic? Why does the longing for guaranteed outcomes hinder our ability to trust God in the immediacy of the moment?

5. Moses feared failure and sought to escape God's call. What failures have you experienced? How could they be God's tools to position you for greater things going forward?

Chapter Four

SINGING OUR WORRIES AND ANXIETIES

My life has been full of terrible misfortunes
most of which never happened.
—Michel de Montaigne

Ray Charles said, "Music is powerful. As people listen to it, they can be affected. They respond." Aldous Huxley chimed in, saying, "After silence that which comes nearest to expressing the inexpressible is music." Maria von Trapp, made famous in *The Sound of Music*, opined, "Music—what a powerful instrument, what a mighty weapon!"

Little wonder, then, that the largest book in the Bible doubles as a hymnal—a collection of songs that powerfully speak into the experiences of life. But whenever we begin to consider the Psalms, it is helpful to be reminded of what these songs and prayers are all about. As we saw briefly in chapter

1, the Psalms are primarily inspired expressions of the true emotions of the heart, and that is the unique feature of the Psalms—they record honest (though not always appropriate or God-honoring) responses to God and to life.

It is critical to keep in mind that, though the Psalms are an inspired record of those responses, the responses themselves are not necessarily endorsed by God. The Holy Spirit records them so that we can see the human heart as it really is—and often what we see is not a pretty sight! For example, consider the words of Psalm 137:9:

> Blessed will be the one who seizes and
> dashes your children
> Against the rock.

Sung "by the rivers of Babylon" (v. 1), this song captures the psalmist's emotions at being in captivity—and they are the emotions of despair and rage. In fact, a rage so sweeping that it sees the slaughter of small children as both justified and blessed! It is hard to imagine anyone assuming that God approves of such murderous anger. But that isn't the point. The psalm is not about divine approval—it is an inspired account of the singer's true feelings in that particular moment in time.

Perhaps nowhere in the Scriptures do we hear our own worries as fully expressed as we do in the Psalms. These inspired hymns and prayers are a record of how the singers and poets responded to the realities of life's joys and struggles—struggles that are often at the root of our own anxieties. Psalms of worship and celebration respond to the joys of life, but the role of psalms of protest and lament is to respond to the worries and fears of life. We will consider such a song of lament in this chapter, where David's anxiety is, in part, rooted in God's apparent disinterest in his pain.

The Psalms are sometimes joyful, sometimes filled with rage, but—above all else—always honest. Perhaps this is why we so readily retreat to the Psalms in our difficult moments. While the events triggering the Psalms may not have been the same as our experiences, the psalmists' emotions often resonate deeply with our own. And that is true when our driving emotion is worry—as it seems to be for David as he sings his worries in Psalm 13.

Background on Psalms

The 150 psalms are divided into five books of psalms (1–41, 42–72, 73–89, 90–106, 107–150) and were written by a wide range of authors over many centuries. While most are attributed to David, other authors include Asaph, the sons of Korah, Heman, Solomon, and even Moses.

While not always the case, many psalms have at their heading (under the psalm number in English translations) a *superscription*. These superscriptions often contain an attribution of authorship, musical instructions on how the song was to be presented, and, with a number of David's psalms in particular, a brief description of the events that prompted the writing of the psalm.

Unsurprisingly, due in part to the versatile nature of

music and in part to the overall scope of the book, there are many different types, or genres, of psalms. As with literature, genres are categories of differing types of content. In literature, you have categories like fiction, nonfiction, science fiction, biography, fantasy, romance, history, and much more. With the Psalms, the genres include creation, wisdom, salvation history (how God rescued Israel from Egypt), worship, thanksgiving, and more. As we mentioned earlier, our focus in this chapter is on the genre of lament.

Lament psalms form the most numerous genre in the book—42 of the 150 songs or over 25 percent of the Psalter. This is especially true among the psalms of David—including the psalm we will consider here: Psalm 13.

Old Testament professor David Lamb says that there are five components to a lament psalm: invocation, complaint, petition, trust, and praise. In fact, Lamb suggests that Psalm 13 follows and is almost prototypical of this pattern of lament psalms. The invocation is in verse 1 (speaking directly to the Lord himself), the complaint encompasses verses 1 and 2, the petition is found in verses 3 and 4, the trust is expressed in verse 5, and the anticipation of praise is affirmed in verse 6. With some minor variations, we will consider Psalm 13 according to this structure.

Song of Protest

Yes, as Ray Charles said, "Music is powerful."

We could think of a number of motivations for writing a song—love, rejection, celebration, loneliness, and so on. But one motivation that might not immediately come to mind is that of protest. My generation will remember, however, during the Vietnam War, the various protest songs that rang out in opposition to that controversial conflict:

"For What It's Worth" by Buffalo Springfield

"Give Peace a Chance" by the Plastic Ono Band (John Lennon)

"Fortunate Son" by Creedence Clearwater Revival

"Masters of War" by Bob Dylan

"Something in the Air" by Thunderclap Newman

"American Woman" by the Guess Who

While some saw such songs as unpatriotic at the least and perhaps giving aid and comfort to the enemy at the most, the writers of these songs saw what they considered an intolerable situation and protested with the visceral songs that sprang from their hearts and minds. I don't know if they had any hope that their songs would make a difference in the global situation, but they sang their protests nonetheless—and those protests resonated with the hearts of many young people of that day.

In Psalm 13, David makes his own protest in the form of a complaint in this song of lament. Notice how the song opens:

How long, LORD? Will You forget me forever?

How long will You hide Your face from me?
How long am I to feel anxious in my soul,
With grief in my heart all the day?
How long will my enemy be exalted over
    me? (vv. 1–2)

This level of protest from David is not at all a shock. Again, complaint is a standard component to a song of lament. And in this case, though David's complaint is secondarily against his enemies and the way they are threatening him, his primary complaint is against God himself (v. 1)! Encapsulated in the fourfold complaint "how long" is David's response to God's seeming indifference to his situation.

I think that, though we might try to express it in a more socially acceptable way, all of us have had moments when we wondered why God wasn't showing up in the midst of our own struggles. The phrase "how long" can easily be sprinkled into our prayers—expressing the same emotional struggles that David was facing.

He felt forgotten (v. 1).

He felt as if God were hiding from him (v. 1).

He felt abandoned to his own devices (v. 2).

He felt continual sorrow (v. 2).

Bible scholar Allen P. Ross wrote of David's emotions here:

> David felt ignored by God and forgotten. Would this continue indefinitely? Wrestling

inwardly (*with my thoughts* is lit., "in my soul"), David lamented that he spent *every day* in this distressing situation, that his *heart* was filled with struggles and *sorrow*. As a result of his apparently being forsaken by God, his enemies triumphed *over* him.

James E. Smith went even further—attaching anxiety to David's appeal, entitling this psalm as "Overcoming Anxiety":

Ps[alm] 13 reflects the anxiety of David when he was in flight from Saul. The language is general but one foe in particular stands out above the rest.

Admittedly, it is unclear whether or not Saul is the particular foe in view since the superscription doesn't tell us. What is abundantly clear, however, is that David is worried about the situation—and his anxieties are compounded by the silence and perceived absence of God. He clearly doesn't know how long he will be able to hold up without God's intervention on his behalf. So his mounting anxiety voices itself in a complaint against God himself!

Have you ever felt that way? If so, you are in good company.

In a boat on the stormy Sea of Galilee, the disciples cried to Jesus (asleep in the boat), "Teacher, do You not care that we are perishing?" (Mark 4:38).

In a home filled with people, an overwhelmed Martha

asked Jesus, "Lord, do You not care that my sister has left me to do the serving by myself? Then tell her to help me" (Luke 10:40).

"Lord, do you not care?" is the New Testament equivalent to David's "How long, LORD?" It is an honest expression of those who feel that they have been abandoned, forsaken, yes, even forgotten by God himself.

Even the perfect Son of God declared from the cross, "'Eli, Eli, lema sabaktanei?' that is, 'My God, My God, why have You forsaken Me?'" (Matthew 27:46).

Yes, even our Lord himself expressed the sense of abandonment that can overtake us when we are engulfed by pressure or problems or people. And while our tendency is to jump immediately to the solution by remembering God's promise, "I will never desert you, nor will I ever abandon you" (Hebrews 13:5), sometimes it can be instructive to sit in the emotional tension of feeling forgotten or alone. No, He will never leave us or forsake us—but sometimes it can feel as if that is exactly what has happened. And that is where David is as he opens Psalm 13.

Song of Appeal

But while we often feel the legitimate need for complaint, that is not where we should stay. As English minister William L. Watkinson said, "Yet is it better to light the candle than to curse the darkness." The point? Don't just complain—do something!

Frankly, there are times I don't want to hear that. I

want to wallow in my despair and self-pity and complaint rather than look to my wise heavenly Father and look for His good purposes in my season of struggle.

David doesn't just complain either. He lights his own candle by continuing to believe that God is able to come to his rescue—and embodies that confidence in a dramatic appeal to his seemingly silent God.

> Consider and answer me, O LORD my God;
> Enlighten my eyes, or I will sleep the sleep
> of death. (Psalm 13:3)

To express this appeal in modern language, David is asking God to pay attention to his despair. In spite of his anxieties and worries, David still has hope that God has not utterly forsaken him. So he expresses his requests, including an appeal for enlightenment. Apart from God's help and guidance, the overwhelmed psalmist will ultimately be crushed and killed.

As a result, David seeks God's response in different ways. First, he asks God to "consider"—that is, to look, to see, to pay attention to the singer's dilemma. Here David is expressing a thought similar to that found in Psalm 35:22:

> You have seen it, LORD, do not keep silent;
> Lord, do not be far from me.

If God will but consider David's situation, it is hard to imagine that He wouldn't respond.

This is a pattern we see consistently in the New

Testament—sight produces an emotional reaction which delivers an active response. Notice Matthew 9:36:

> Seeing the crowds, He felt compassion for them, because they were distressed and downcast, like sheep without a shepherd.

Jesus saw the condition of the crowds, He felt compassion for them, and He called His disciples to pray for the Father to send laborers into the harvest (v. 38). Knowing the Father's love for him, David just wants Him to see the problem, knowing that it will elicit a response.

Then David prays for God to "enlighten [his] eyes" (Psalm 13:3). It seems to speak of granting him the light of wisdom so that David can best respond to the challenges he faces.

And if God doesn't respond? David expresses the nature of his fear and anxiety:

> And my enemy will say, "I have overcome
>   him,"
> And my adversaries will rejoice when I am
>   shaken. (v. 4)

If God doesn't come to David's aid, the singer's worst fears will be realized—his worries will actually come true in his life and his enemies will gain the ultimate advantage over him. Willem VanGemeren summed up Psalm 13 well:

> This psalm, which is a deeply moving picture of despair and trust, realistically

depicts the anguish of the soul, yet is characteristic of a life of deep faith.

Song of Deliberate Trust

When I was a boy, the schoolyard was the place where bullies threw their weight around and kids like me received that bullying with minimal protest. As we cowered in fear before our tormenters, the part of the bullying that was almost the worst of all was when they would press the "fear button" with taunting comments:

> Are you scared?
> You're afraid of me, aren't you?
> There's no one here to protect you . . . What are you going to do now?

In fact, most of those times I really *was* frightened—and with good cause. Having been punched senseless in the past, the one thing you know in that moment is that you don't want to experience that again. So what do you do and who can you trust when you are paralyzed with fear? When you're eight years old and being bullied by a kid who is older, bigger, and stronger, fear is legitimate and real.

Not much has changed since those days of boyhood struggle. As we saw in an earlier chapter, fear is an almost ever-present reality in today's world—and it can come at us from a variety of directions.

So what is the bottom line?

Fear is an emotional response to a known or definite
  threat.

Anxiety is a diffuse, unpleasant, vague sense of appre-
  hension.

To see these emotions in operation, we return to David's Psalm 13, where we have heard his fears but have felt
his anxieties. Yet the consummation of the song is that it
lifts him to a renewed confidence in the God who has not
yet responded to him!

> But I have trusted in Your faithfulness;
> My heart shall rejoice in Your salvation.
> I will sing to the LORD,
> Because He has looked after me. (vv. 5–6)

Notice that, although David's present tense situation
has not changed, he anchors his hope for the future in his
experiences with God in the past. "I have trusted" is a re-
flection on past trials and God's faithful response to them.

The classic example from David's life, seen earlier, came
when he was but a lad, volunteering to face off with the
giant Philistine warrior Goliath. David's age and lack of
experience brought the entire situation into question, so
David responded with stories of God's faithfulness:

> But Saul said to David, "You are not able
> to go against this Philistine to fight him;
> for you are only a youth, while he has
> been a warrior since his youth." But David

said to Saul, "Your servant was tending his father's sheep. When a lion or a bear came and took a sheep from the flock, I went out after it and attacked it, and rescued the sheep from its mouth; and when it rose up against me, I grabbed it by its mane and struck it and killed it. Your servant has killed both the lion and the bear; and this uncircumcised Philistine will be like one of them, since he has defied the armies of the living God." And David said, "The LORD who saved me from the paw of the lion and the paw of the bear, He will save me from the hand of this Philistine." So Saul said to David, "Go, and may the LORD be with you." (1 Samuel 17:33–37)

Reflecting on God's rescue in the past positioned David to trust God for His help in the present situation—and set the stage for a glad celebration to come! He is saying, "I have trusted," and "I will rejoice and I will sing" (see Psalm 13:5–6). What a contrast to the despair of verses 1 and 2 as David not only anticipates God's deliverance and rescue but also looks forward to celebrating that rescue in worship and praise.

Song of Anticipated Praise

I can't even count the number of times I have been in a prayer meeting when, after a boatload of requests have been lifted to the throne of God, someone intones, "God, we thank you in advance for what you are going to do."

That requires a measure of faith, doesn't it? How easy it is to praise God after the outcome has been settled, but how hard it is to trust God so implicitly that we praise him for outcomes that are yet unrealized. Often the key to that kind of praise is basing our hopes of what is to come on what has been. Focusing on God's track record of past faithfulness allows us to worship in the messy present tense before hopes have been realized.

In the Goliath incident, David based his expectations of God's work in the present on how God had acted in the past. Here in Psalm 13, it feels as if he is doing a similar thing. His confidence in God is not rooted in God's apparent inactivity in the present but in His past deliverances. This leads to the praise and worship David anticipates giving to God in verse 6:

> I will sing to the LORD,
> Because He has looked after me.

What a contrast to how this song of lament began! This contrast is one of the defining differences between a song of complaint and a proper lament—a lament is not the end of the story or of the song. Lament is one step in the process that leads from despair to hope. From complaint to worship. From anxiety to trust. Lament is not just about venting your anger or frustration—lament is intended to take you beyond a point of fear, worry, or anxiety to reasons for hope and purposeful praise.

In an individual lament like Psalm 13, the singer's fears, anxieties, and worries are real—but so is the legitimate expectation of God's help. As the old hymn by Isaac Watts affirms:

> O God, our help in ages past,
> Our hope for years to come,
> Our shelter from the stormy blast,
> And our eternal home.

The hymn was originally printed in *The Psalms of David: Imitated in the Language of the New Testament, and Apply'd to the Christian State and Worship*, published by Watts in 1719. How appropriate! This great hymn finds its roots in Psalm 90 (which actually was a psalm by Moses rather than David) and reminds us how valuable it is to allow the Scriptures to instruct us on how to express our need for and confidence in God. As David did in Psalm 13, Watts's opening stanza expresses the past, present, future, and, yes, even eternal nature of God's care for us.

And when, in our anxiety-laced, fear-filled experiences, God's past help merges into God's great hope and protection, we have great cause for worship—worship of which God is more than worthy.

Questions for Personal Reflection or Group Discussion

1. Do you have a favorite psalm? If so, what is it and why do you find it so meaningful?

2. Which genre in the Psalms do you find yourself drawn to? Why?

3. In David's lament of Psalm 13, he complains of God's apparent absence during his season of struggle and need. Think about a time when you felt similarly. How did God ultimately show himself to be faithful—in spite of what had seemed to be His disinterest?

4. One significant difference between a lament psalm and a general complaint is that lament leads us to see God as trustworthy—rather than leaving us in despair. Do you find it difficult to make that transition from complaint to trust? Why or why not?

5. Think about a time when God showed His faithfulness to you in some tangible way—perhaps an answer to prayer or an unexpected provision. How can that memory of God's past faithfulness strengthen your trust in Him during more current struggles?

Chapter Five

SPEAKING WORDS OF WISDOM

So do not worry about tomorrow; for tomorrow will worry about itself. Each day has enough trouble of its own.

—Jesus of Nazareth (Matthew 6:34)

Authorities. The media is filled with so-called experts who are supposed to give us enhanced understanding of complex or challenging situations. Turn to any cable news network and, whatever the issue or event may be that they are covering, they will have authorities address that issue. If it is a conflict situation, there will be some retired army general providing insight on the military exercise. If it is a medical situation, doctors and scientists will be called upon to make the matter understandable, or at least relatable. When matters of the economy are in view, some financial guru plays the role of Wall Street analyst and steps in to unravel the mysteries of global economics.

Even sports shows are packed with former players and coaches—all of whom are there to give us some inside information. Many football fans today are not even aware that, years ago, the late John Madden was a Super Bowl–winning head coach. They know Madden for his television commentary on football games and, even more, for his NFL-based video games. Likewise, Johnny Miller was one of the greatest golfers of his generation. Modern golf fans, however, know him better as a recently retired golf analyst on NBC.

It seems that no matter where we turn, there is an authority. An expert. A wise old head to guide our way through the gnarly situations of life—or at least the ones in which we are interested. Even in spiritual matters, many of us have favorite Bible teachers or pastors who serve as authorities on Scripture or scriptural matters we encounter in our daily living.

But where do we turn when it comes to matters of worry or anxiety? What authoritative voice can we trust to help us unravel our deep-seated fears that can pervade our thinking?

When the Beatles were in the process of unraveling as a musical group, Paul McCartney wrote the now-classic tune "Let It Be." The theme of the song? He was worried about the deteriorating situation in which he and his friends found themselves, and needing wisdom, he wished he could talk to his mother, Mary, who had died when Sir Paul was but a youngster. Similarly, George

Harrison had long since turned to an Indian guru to help guide him through life's ups and downs.

But where can *we* turn? I would suggest that in matters of worry—or anything else in life for that matter—we turn to Jesus, the one who has been made for us to be "wisdom from God" (1 Corinthians 1:30). The one best able to advise us because He fully and intimately knows the Father and how our God can equip us to respond to life's darker moments. Jesus is our ultimate authority, and to hear His perfectly wise counsel, we turn to the Sermon on the Mount and Jesus's teaching on wisdom versus worry in Matthew 6:24–34. In that teaching, our Lord addresses several key issues we will consider together.

The Context of Jesus's Teaching

When we turn to the Sermon on the Mount, we are joining Jesus in the earliest stages of His public ministry. In Matthew 4:17, that ministry had begun with Jesus's announcement that the "kingdom of heaven is at hand" followed by the selection of His first disciples (vv. 18–22) and an early round of healings (vv. 23–25).

Those events were then followed by the Sermon on the Mount. This message serves a dual purpose in Matthew's gospel. First, it is the first of five major teaching blocks that Jesus delivers in Matthew's gospel. Those five major messages form the spine of Matthew's telling of Jesus's story. But the second purpose speaks into our purposes here. Having announced that the kingdom of heaven has arrived (specifically arriving in the presence of the King himself—Jesus), our Lord then proceeds to explain what life in His kingdom looks like. The key here is that the Greek word for "kingdom" (*basileia*) is not a reference to an institutional kingdom but rather speaks to God's rule and authority. A life in His kingdom is a life under His rule—and by definition that rule will be qualitatively different from any kingdom or ruling authority the world has ever known. Followers of Christ are citizens of His kingdom living under His rule, as Paul told the church at Colossae:

> For He rescued us from the domain of darkness, and transferred us to the kingdom of His beloved Son. (Colossians 1:13)

The Sermon on the Mount gives us guidelines for living as citizens of Jesus's own kingdom. And in the heart of that message, those guidelines offer words of divine wisdom for seasons of anxiety and worry.

Issues of Worldview

A word that I first became aware of in the early 1990s that has since solidly lodged itself into our collective consciousness is the term *worldview*. Whether that worldview is secular, socialist, or biblically Christian, it is the lens through which life is not only viewed but understood and interpreted.

In this light, Jesus situated His words of wisdom about

worry with some words that comfortably fit into the concept of worldview. Notice Matthew 6:24:

> No one can serve two masters; for either
> he will hate the one and love the other, or
> he will be devoted to one and despise the
> other. You cannot serve God and wealth.

A substantial part of worldview is that it speaks to what we value—and in much of today's world that value is defined by dollar signs. Jesus attacked that worldview head-on, declaring that only one thing should dominate us. Rule us. To use Jesus's own word, *master* us, which the Jamieson, Fausset, and Brown *A Commentary, Critical and Explanatory, on the Whole Bible* says means "belong wholly and be entirely under command to." Jesus is asserting that only one thing can be the object of our service. You can only be wholly and entirely commanded by one—and Jesus says that the primary choices are God and wealth, whether in the form of property, possessions, or money.

Our worldview reflects what we value—and that question becomes all the more significant when we must wrestle with the issue of who or what we will serve. And Jesus lifts up the problem of wealth as a primary threat to our service of God himself. Warren Wiersbe wisely commented on Jesus's words this way:

> We are accustomed to dividing life into
> the "spiritual" and the "material"; but Jesus

made no such division. In many of His parables, He made it clear that a right attitude toward wealth is a mark of true spirituality (see Luke 12:13ff; 16:1–31). The Pharisees were covetous (Luke 16:14) and used religion to make money. If we have the true righteousness of Christ in our lives, then we will have a proper attitude toward material wealth.

Hear his words: "a right attitude toward wealth is a mark of true spirituality." And that attitude is the very essence of a biblical worldview, echoing Paul's words to the church at Philippi, "Have this attitude in yourselves which was also in Christ Jesus . . ." (Philippians 2:5). Paul then goes on to define that attitude as Jesus's willingness to sacrifice all in order to accomplish the Father's purposes.

This is critically important. When Jesus was teaching in Matthew 6, His words were the absolute opposite of theoretical. Jesus's very presence on this earth showed that He valued the Father more than His own royal position—choosing not to selfishly cling to His privileges as the second person of the Trinity (Philippians 2:6) but instead to serve the Father by coming to earth: "He humbled Himself by becoming obedient to the point of death: death on a cross" (v. 8).

If worldview reveals what we value, then Jesus's worldview was one in which He supremely valued the Father and His priorities—which included self-sacrifice in order to rescue us. Talk about a worldview: "God so loved the world" (John 3:16).

Now, it is vital that we recognize that just as worldview was not theoretical for Jesus, it should not be theoretical for us either. And especially as it relates to money, this worldview statement from our Lord in Matthew 6:24 leads to His wisdom on worry.

The Nature of Worry

When I was a boy, my dad—at forty-two years of age— had his first major heart attack. In the days that followed, his doctor, Dr. Vail, visited him in his hospital room and coached him on the nature of his heart problem and the probable causes of that issue. This was necessary because, if Dad was going to battle this problem, he needed, as much as possible, to understand it. That understanding led to some rather substantial lifestyle changes—including stopping smoking and changing his dietary norms. These changes defined the rest of Dad's life because he trusted Dr. Vail and because he acted on the understanding the good doctor imparted to him.

This is exactly what Jesus does in the Sermon on the Mount. After explaining the nature of money in our worldview, our Lord goes on to explain the nature of the problem of worry. Notice Matthew 6:25:

> For this reason I say to you, do not be worried about your life, as to what you will

eat or what you will drink; nor for your body, as to what you will put on. Is life not more than food, and the body more than clothing?

Notice how Jesus's explanation of the nature of worry connects to the worldview statement of serving wealth by the words "for this reason." Jesus is about to talk about worry because of our attitudes toward money. Why? Perhaps it is because of the nature of the things we tend to worry about. Our Lord lists the basic necessities of life—nourishment and covering for our bodies. We could certainly add housing and other similar things, but Jesus's words aim at our most core concerns—the things that are necessary for health and well-being. These are, by extension, the things that money can buy. If we are trusting in money to meet our most basic needs, then we have much to worry about. But Jesus strongly challenges this trust in money, connecting the concerns about worldview with the concerns about worry—through that statement "for this reason."

To be sure, basic needs are not the only things we tend to worry about. Anyone who travels internationally knows the tension we can experience over flight delays, with the resulting missed connections that can trickle down to cause huge problems on the other end. On one particular trip to South America, a series of delays caused me to arrive a full day late. That meant that I missed my first speaking opportunity scheduled on the trip, at which I would have had the privilege of addressing several thousand pastors. As it was, when I arrived, we loaded up a car for a six-hour drive to the next speaking engagement, where, upon arrival, I literally walked right onto the platform, was introduced to my interpreter, and began teaching. A few of those situations and you find yourself repeatedly wondering if flights will be on time and connections will be made. Delays are worrisome.

We also can find ourselves worrying about relationships. "Will that person be faithful?" we ask, while it is quite likely that the other person is wondering the same thing about us. We worry that perhaps we are making ourselves terribly vulnerable by giving our heart to someone—knowing that relationships break, marriages fail, and trusts are broken every day. We worry as we wonder, Who can I really trust?

Yes, while Jesus directly addressed the fundamental basics of life (food, clothing), our worries are not limited to those basics. We worry about the complexities of life on both a personal and a global level. In the micro of our personal lives, we tend to worry about our marriages, our kids, our jobs, and our finances, while in the macro of life, we worry about global conflicts, pandemics, financial meltdowns, and terrorism.

Yet we must hear Jesus's words of challenge: "Is life not more than food, and the body more than clothing?" Those things may impact our lives—even dramatically— but His assertion is that life is more than those things. Why? Because God is the source and author of life—and He can be trusted to care for that life. And that is the point Jesus makes next.

Lessons from Nature

Debates over the origins of life have been raging ever since Charles Darwin boarded the ship the HMS *Beagle* and headed out to find evidence for what would become known as the theory of evolution. Meanwhile advocates of creation (sometimes referred to as intelligent design) continued to argue for a Creator who made all the things that we see and made them with intentionality and purpose. As time has passed, more and more ideas have been added to the debate including the big bang, spontaneous origin, and even extraterrestrial activity—perhaps life on our world came from debris from another planet.

In a sense, as Jesus continued His argument against worry, He made a passive argument for the Creator. Notice that embedded within the idea of God as Creator is the underlying reality of God as Sustainer, found in Matthew 6:26–30:

> Look at the birds of the sky, that they do not sow, nor reap, nor gather crops into barns, and yet your heavenly Father feeds them. Are you not much more important than they? And which of you by worrying can add a single day to his life's span? And why are you worried about clothing? Notice how the lilies of the field grow; they do not labor nor do they spin thread for cloth, yet I say to you that not even

Solomon in all his glory clothed himself like one of these. But if God so clothes the grass of the field, which is alive today and tomorrow is thrown into the furnace, will He not much more clothe you? You of little faith!

Jesus argued that the Creator is responsible for caring for His creation—something that is evidenced by creation itself. The birds and flowers are dependent upon God for their well-being—and Jesus maintained that you and I are worth much more than those things! Pastor Warren Wiersbe wrote wisely of these words:

> We may dignify worry by calling it by some other name—concern, burden, a cross to bear—but the results are still the same. Instead of helping us live longer, anxiety only makes life shorter (Matt. 6:27). The Greek word translated "take no thought" literally means "to be drawn in different directions." Worry pulls us apart. Until man interferes, everything in nature works together, because all of nature trusts God. Man, however, is pulled apart because he tries to live his own life by depending on material wealth.

We are "pulled apart" by a worry not manifested in nature—and the reason we are pulled apart is that we are not trusting our Creator to care for us. We just struggle to believe that God cares for us as much as He does. But Jesus makes it clear that God's heart is for us—He really does care, and the extent of that care is evidenced in the cross itself. Yet somehow we find it easy to believe that God cares deeply for our eternity but perhaps not as much for our here and now. As hymn writer Etta Lewis expressed it:

> He careth for me, my Father cares!
> Oh, sweetest tho't to my spirit known;
> I have no fears for the coming years,
> He ne'er forsakes me nor leaves His own.

> "He careth for me,"—my morning hymn,
> "He careth for me,"—my evening psalm;
> By day, by night, in glom, in light,
> Beneath is the everlasting arm.

The One who made us for himself will care for us, and we can trust Him for that provision. This, the writer of the letter to the Hebrews says, is in part why we pray:

> Therefore let's approach the throne of grace with confidence, so that we may receive mercy and find grace for help at the time of our need. (4:16)

In our time of need, we pray—even if it is only for our daily bread (Matthew 6:11) and the basics of life.

Our Basis for Confident Trust

Are you familiar with the term *practical atheism*? It is a very real thing. Psalm 14:1 asserts that "the fool has said in his heart, 'There is no God.'" With the evidence of creation that surrounds us, it is easy to see the point the psalmist is making. But atheism is different from *practical* atheism. How? An atheist believes there is no god, so by definition you can't be an atheist and a believer in Jesus. A practical atheist, however, *lives* as if there is no God—and many of us, in spite of being followers of Christ, live that way day in and day out.

Where does that fit in a conversation on worry? Jesus says that worry causes us to live like "Gentiles," here meaning those people who don't know God. Those who don't have a relationship with the true and living God who can be trusted. Rather than living a life of worry as if there is no God, we can learn from Jesus's words:

> Do not worry then, saying, "What are we to eat?" or "What are we to drink?" or "What are we to wear for clothing?" For the Gentiles eagerly seek all these things; for your heavenly Father knows that you need all these things. But seek first His kingdom and His righteousness, and all these things will be provided to you.
>
> So do not worry about tomorrow; for tomorrow will worry about itself. Each day

has enough trouble of its own. (Matthew 6:31–34)

Rather than following the example of the Gentiles who don't know God, we are called by Jesus to follow the example of nature which experiences God's provision and doesn't fret. Writing in *The Bible Knowledge Commentary*, L. A. Barbieri Jr. wrote:

> Rather than being like **the pagans** who are concerned about physical needs, the Lord's disciples should be concerned about the things of God, **His kingdom and His righteousness.** Then **all these needs will be** supplied in God's timing. This is the life of daily faith. It does no good to worry—**do not worry** occurs three times (vv. 25, 31, 34; cf. vv. 27–28)—or be concerned **about tomorrow for** there are sufficient matters to attend to **each day.**

In a sense, we have more important matters to concern us—matters that relate to God's kingdom and righteousness (right standing with God). R. T. France, in *The New Bible Commentary*, agreed:

> There is a beautiful simplicity about vs 25–33, with their appeal to the example of the birds and flowers to illustrate God's lavish care for all his creatures. What is forbidden

here is *worry*, not responsible provision for one's own and one's family needs; God provides food for *the birds*, but they still have to search for it! The basis of the disciple's confidence, in contrast with the anxiety of *the pagans*, lies in recognizing God as *your heavenly Father* (32). The proper attitude then is to put God first (33) and to trust him for our practical needs.

I like that—put God first and then trust Him. That, by the way, is the very opposite of practical atheism because it is a life that not only lives as if there is a God but lives as if the reality of God is the most important of all realities. As a result, trust is seen as the answer to worry.

When we know God and trust God, worry becomes redundant. As Jesus said, it can't accomplish anything, but it can be very destructive. Trusting God, however, is at the heart of shalom—the peace that all is well because God is in control and He is the heavenly Father to whom we pray. As Joachim Neander wrote in the classic hymn "Praise to the Lord, the Almighty":

> Praise to the Lord, who o'er all things so
>   wondrously reigneth,
> Shelters thee under his wings, yea, so gen-
>   tly sustaineth!
> Hast thou not seen how thy desires e'er
>   have been
> Granted in what he ordaineth?

Questions for Personal Reflection or Group Discussion

1. What are some areas in life where you find yourself prone to worry? Why do those areas seem to affect you so much?

2. How does Jesus's argument about who or what you serve (God or money) address many of the pressures of modern culture and that culture's worldview?

3. What does the example of the lilies of the field and the birds of the air teach us about our Creator?

4. What makes it challenging to trust God and put Him first? How can prayer help us in that challenge?

Chapter Six

WALLS TO LEAN ON

Anxiety in a person's heart weighs it down,
But a good word makes it glad.
—Proverbs 12:25

Walls are interesting things. In 1961, I was a boy when the news arrived that the city of Berlin, Germany, was being divided by the now-infamous Berlin Wall—a wall that would remain in place for some twenty-eight years until its demolition in 1989. This wall created such a huge focal point to the struggle for freedom in that divided city that, two years later in 1963, American president John Kennedy empathized with those beleaguered Berliners with the now-famous words, "Ich bin ein Berliner" ("I am a Berliner"), and twenty-four years after that in 1987, President Ronald Reagan challenged the Soviet Union's leader with the words, "Mr. Gorbachev, tear down this wall." Two years later the wall would fall—but not as a result of the action of governments. It fell as the result of a grassroots movement that would no longer abide such a tyrannical monument.

The most famous wall of ancient times—and still today in Asia—is of course the Great Wall of China. However, while the Berlin Wall was erected to keep people *in*, the Great Wall was apparently constructed to keep potential invaders *out* and to control borders so that trade goods could be taxed upon entering the country. So not all walls have evil intent attached to them. Some are recognized as providing a very important service—security.

In our homes, walls divide spaces, but even more they *define* those spaces. But in today's style preferences, more and more people want fewer and fewer walls, instead seeking what is known as an open concept for their homes. Again, walls being depicted in a negative context.

It is with similar negative views that people have commented on walls:

> "Nothing kills creativity faster than a wall." —Eric Weiner

> "Men build too many walls and not enough bridges." —Joseph Fort Newton

Even the Bible's most familiar story about walls concludes with a trumpet blast and "the walls came a-tumbling down."

But what are the benefits of walls—other than attempted security? When I was in junior high, about once a month the school sponsored a sock hop. (For my younger readers, it was an afternoon dance held in the school gym, but you couldn't wear shoes on the gym floor—hence the word *sock*). The gym walls provided a huge service as one side of the gym was filled with girls leaning against the wall while the boys stood on the other side. Those who weren't invited to dance were called, appropriately, wallflowers. As we lined those walls, they gave us the opportunity to be present but also gave us support in those long moments of being ignored while we waited to be invited to join in the fun. In essence, the walls gave us some visible means of support. Something to lean on.

I would suggest that walls can still remind us of supportive elements that can strengthen us in times when we feel weak or, as we have been considering in this book, worried. Having something to lean on when our world is feeling a bit shaky with anxiety can be a great help and encouragement.

Where can we find strength when worry threatens to overwhelm us? As we come to the conclusion of this book, it is not my intent to just simply say, "Don't worry, be happy," as the Bobby McFerrin song put it. What I would suggest instead, and suggest rather strongly, is that when our spiritual knees are shaken with worry and distress, the Scriptures offer us some very helpful walls to lean on. Let's consider them now.

The Heart of God

In the exodus experience of Israel, God rescued His chosen people from centuries of slavery in Egypt and led them to the base of Mount Sinai. There God introduced himself to them and called them to be His people—and to worship none other than himself. Their response?

> Then Moses came and reported to the people all the words of the LORD and all the ordinances; and all the people answered with one voice and said, "All the words which the LORD has spoken we will do!" (Exodus 24:3)

The people promised, "We'll do everything God asked." But exactly eight chapters and one golden calf later, the people of Israel were worshipping a golden calf—crafted by, of all people, Aaron, their newly appointed high priest. When Moses returned to the mountaintop to meet God after this massive disobedience, he could have been forgiven for perhaps expecting God to respond with anger and judgment. Instead, God told Moses of His heart for those disobedient people:

> Then the LORD passed by in front of him and proclaimed, "The LORD, the LORD God, compassionate and merciful, slow to anger, and abounding in faithfulness and truth; who keeps faithfulness for thousands, who forgives wrongdoing, violation of His Law, and sin; yet He will by no means leave the guilty unpunished." (Exodus 34:6–7)

Yes, God will deal with sin and wrongdoing—but His heart is one of mercy, grace, and love. Peter put it ever so simply when he affirmed, "Cast all your anxiety on Him, because He cares about you" (1 Peter 5:7).

Even when I fail? Yes.

Even when I fear? Yes.

Even when it feels like worries will consume me? Yes.

We are invited to lean against the wall of God's heart, as He invites us to cast all of our anxiety on Him. We must never forget that all of those things that feed our worries are things that He cares about because of His great heart for us. He cares for you. Therefore, He cares about the things that you care about.

In fact, in His parable of the sower and the soils, Jesus acknowledged the reality of those cares and their power, saying, "And the cares of this world, the deceitfulness of riches, and the desires for other things entering in choke the word, and it becomes unfruitful" (Mark 4:19 NKJV).

The cares of this world can be so overwhelming, so life impacting, so debilitating that they can choke out the wooing of the gospel in a person's heart. But, as Peter said, we don't have to live under that burden of anxiety—we can cast it onto our God who cares deeply and greatly for us.

The Availability of God

Bookstores—both physical and digital bookstores—are flooded with how-to books. How to train your dog. How to wire the electrical circuits in a house. How to get a book published (imagine that!). How to speak Mandarin. How to hit a golf shot. The themes are virtually endless. In fact, for the timid of heart who need things simplified, there are the For Dummies books. *German for Dummies. Laptops for Dummies. Taxes for Dummies.* Even *Low-Carb Dieting for Dummies.*

For everything that can be done, there are people who want to know how to do it. I would suggest that some of you who are reading this may have come out of the last section about trusting God's heart and casting your cares on Him wondering, Yes, but how?

The good news is that, while Peter offered us the encouragement to trust God, Paul offers us the how-to in Philippians 4:

> Do not be anxious about anything, but in everything by prayer and pleading with thanksgiving let your requests be made known to God. And the peace of God, which surpasses all comprehension, will guard your hearts and minds in Christ Jesus. (vv. 6–7)

Notice Paul's lead. "Do not be anxious about anything." The Christian Standard Bible translates that phrase, "Don't worry about anything." And A. T. Robertson in his *Word Pictures in the New Testament* puts it equally bluntly, translating it, "Don't worry about anything."

I know—easier said than done, right? But Paul not

only challenges us to abandon the work of worry but also points us to something constructive that can actually make a difference. He calls us to prayer. *Wuest's Word Studies from the Greek New Testament* adds:

> The Greek word here is found in an early manuscript in the sentence, "I am writing in haste to prevent your being anxious, for I will see that you are not worried," where its translation, "anxious" is used as a synonym for the Greek word "worried." The word means "worry, anxious care." The Greek construction indicates that we have here a prohibition which forbids the continuance of an action already habitually going on. The Philippian saints were habitually worrying. Paul exhorts them to stop it. The word "nothing" is literally "not even one thing."

When we face fears, threats (real or imagined), or the unknown, entrusting those challenges to God in prayer is a positive act. And this is important because the challenge to stop worrying is not a call to apathy, indifference, or simply not caring. It raises the bar even higher because not only do we care; we care enough to take these burdens to the Creator of the universe! As Peter's response to the cares of this life is to trust God, Paul's method for implementing that trust is prayer. Bible scholar J. A. Bengel said, "Anxiety and prayer are more opposed to each other than fire and water."

In *The Expositor's Bible Commentary*, D. E. Garland wrote, "They are to 'present [their] requests to God,' not because God is unaware of their needs and needs to be informed, but because it is a way to acknowledge their total dependence on God." This is an important reminder for us. Yes, God is always fully aware of what we need and what concerns us. But are we always fully aware of how much we need Him? Sometimes it is only in the crucible of deep difficulties that we once again embrace our deep reliance upon our Father and embrace that reliance through prayer.

As one scholar put it, "The way to worry about nothing is to pray about everything!" And what are the characteristics of that prayer? Paul lists three aspects of prayer to be included when we are struggling with worries and cares.

Worship. Some see the Greek word here as general prayer for the general things of life. Warren Wiersbe wrote in *Be Joyful*, his brief commentary on Philippians, "The word *prayer* is the general word for making requests known to the Lord. It carries the idea of adoration, devotion, and worship." These prayers seem to include the acknowledgment of who God is and why He is so worthy of our love and worship. These general prayers are followed by pleading.

Pleading. Here is the kind of prayer that is seeking a specific response to a specific need—like when a specific care is weighing down your heart and mind to the point that you can't sleep. I get it. Our oldest son enlisted in the US Army shortly after the 9/11 attacks and, immediately following his completion of basic training, was deployed to Afghanistan. For Marlene and me, it was a long deployment filled with wondering about what could happen to our son. In the years since he left the Army, he has told us just enough stories of his time in Afghanistan, followed by two deployments to Iraq, for us to know that our concerns were not unfounded. During those months, we made very specific prayers for Matt, and thankfully he made it home every time. Thankfully.

Thanksgiving. Giving thanks may be a surprising third characteristic of our prayers, given the nature of the way worry impacts our thinking. But remembering to give thanks is anything but surprising if we think about it for five seconds. When we give thanks we are not only praising God for what He has done for us but reminding ourselves of His acts on our behalf! Practicing prayers of thanksgiving is one of the most faith-enriching things we can do. Johnson Oatman's classic hymn puts it well:

> When upon life's billows you are tempest
>   tossed,
> When you are discouraged, thinking all is
>   lost,
> Count your many blessings, name them
>   one by one,
> And it will surprise you what the Lord
>   hath done.
>
> Count your blessings, name them one by
>   one;

> Count your blessings, see what God hath
>   done;
> Count your blessings, name them one by
>   one;
> Count your many blessings, see what God
>   hath done.

Where once was worry, now are reminders of God's faithful care for us—and that faithfulness is a major brick in the next wall we can lean against.

The Provision of God

When we pray with supplication and thanksgiving, how might God's care for us be realized or enacted? One possibility comes from the apostle Paul in his first letter to the church at Corinth.

> No temptation has overtaken you except something common to mankind; and God is faithful, so He will not allow you to be tempted beyond what you are able, but with the temptation will provide the way of escape also, so that you will be able to endure it. (10:13)

Of first importance here is that the word *temptation* does not refer to a temptation to sin but rather to a test that is being faced—the very kind of thing we might be tempted to worry about. When we're facing the common trials of life, God will make a way of escape for his children, which the Jamieson, Fausset, and Brown commentary describes this way:

> The *Greek* is, "*the* way of escape"; the appropriate way of escape in each particular temptation; not an immediate escape, but one in due time, after patience has had her perfect work (James 1:2–4, 12). He "makes" the way of escape simultaneously with the temptation which His providence permissively arranges for His people.

When we're overwhelmed by anxiety, one of our first instincts could be to look for an exit strategy. Paul says, quite simply, God's got this. Trust Him to be faithful.

The Presence of God

I have written many times about my love for world football (soccer)—specifically the Liverpool Football Club. For fans of the beautiful game, especially in the English Premier League, one of the enchanting things about the games are the songs the fans sing as they serenade their heroes on the pitch (field). Almost every team has a variety of songs including songs about the players individually. Some of the songs are about the team's history. But above all else, each team has an anthem that the fans sing as the players stride onto the pitch at the start of the game. And the variety of those anthems ranges from the ridiculous to the sublime.

For example, in the category of the ridiculous, Stoke City—the Potters—has the anthem "Delilah," a song recorded in the 1960s by Tom Jones. Meanwhile, West Ham United, a London-based team, steps onto the pitch to the sounds of "I'm Forever Blowing Bubbles." It makes no sense to me whatsoever how those songs have become team anthems.

On the side of the sublime, West Bromwich Albion fans serenade their players by singing "The Lord's My Shepherd," with the lyrics brandished on the facades of their stadium, the Hawthorns. In my mind, however, no team has a better anthem than Liverpool. I have been thrilled to stand in Anfield stadium, Liverpool's home field, as more than fifty thousand Liverpool supporters joined their voices as one to sing "You'll Never Walk Alone."

Though to some this may seem an overly sentimental tune for a football anthem, it is actually the fans and supporters assuring the players that they are in this together. *Together* is a powerful word because it automatically defeats our sense of isolation when worries overwhelm us. This sense of doing life together is at the heart of the Lord's promise found in Hebrews 13:

> Make sure that your character is free from the love of money, being content with what you have; for He Himself has said, "I will never desert you, nor will I ever abandon you," so that we confidently say, "The Lord is my helper, I will not be afraid. What will man do to me?" (vv. 5–6)

"I will never leave you or forsake you" is God's affirmation that, in all the situations and circumstances of life, we never walk alone.

My favorite Bible character is the Old Testament Joseph—and the critical moments in his story happen in Genesis 39. Having been sold into slavery by his own brothers (Genesis 37), he was purchased by Potiphar, an official in Pharaoh's court functioning in a role some scholars believe to have been the royal executioner. As Genesis 39 unfolds, Joseph began the long struggle of life as a slave. But remarkably, he rose to a level of such responsibility that Potiphar entrusted Joseph with everything he had.

By this time, Joseph had been in Egypt for about ten years, and this was the point where Mrs. Potiphar entered the story, attempting to seduce Joseph. When he refused, she lied about him, and the young Hebrew servant was thrust into prison. Genesis 39 concludes with Joseph imprisoned for being a man of integrity.

That, however, is not the key factor in Joseph's story. Whether he was rising to a position of trust or falling into a prison, there was one consistent theme in Joseph's years of experience in Egypt: the Lord was with him. In all that Joseph endured, he never was alone. Joseph lived in the presence of God, as is expressed no less than four times in Genesis 39 (vv. 2, 3, 21, 23). During Joseph's enslavement and his imprisonment, God's presence never wavered—and Joseph, whose experiences could easily have driven him to deep-seated anxieties, found the faithful and trustworthy presence of his God to be the very support he needed in each and every circumstance. And the way of escape we saw in 1 Corinthians 10:13 was made available to Joseph—in part because, in prison, he met members of Pharoah's court who would eventually be God's instruments for bringing justice and escape to Joseph.

Similarly, in Psalm 23 David faced what he called "the valley of the shadow of death." What got him through that valley? As with Joseph, it was the presence of his God:

> Even though I walk through the valley of
> the shadow of death,
> I fear no evil, for You are with me. (v. 4)

At the end of the day, the reminder of the Scriptures is that, although we may have plenty of *reasons* to fear (and worry), we have no *need* to fear. The Lord our Shepherd is with us.

One of the most startling expressions of God's ability to help us in times of great struggle is found in the now-famous story of Chicago businessman H. G. Spafford. Following the Great Chicago Fire, Spafford sent his wife and daughters to England as reconstruction was taking place in Chicago. However, the ship they were sailing on was wrecked in the Atlantic and all four of Spafford's daughters drowned. His wife was rescued and taken to England, where she sent him a cryptic two-word telegram that read, "Saved alone." Upon hearing of the tragedy, Spafford immediately made arrangements to travel to England to be with her.

In this season of overwhelming grief, Spafford truly

experienced a journey through "the valley of the shadow of death," immeasurably more challenging than what Marlene and I experienced when Matt was in the Army.

Along the way, confident of God's faithful presence even during this tremendous loss, Spafford wrote the lyrics to one of the church's most beloved hymns:

> When peace like a river attendeth my way,
> When sorrows like sea billows roll;
> Whatever my lot, Thou hast taught me to
>   say,
> "It is well, it is well with my soul."
>
> It is well (it is well)
> With my soul (with my soul),
> It is well, it is well with my soul.

Only a life lived in the presence of God can know that kind of peace—the peace that surpasses understanding, that God answers with when we pray about our worries and anxieties. "Whatever my lot," the Lord is with me. I don't need to worry. I can lean on Him.

Questions for Personal Reflection or Group Discussion

1. Do you see walls as positives or negatives? Why? Give some examples.

2. When you "cast all your anxiety on Him" (1 Peter 5:7), do you struggle with wanting to take it back? To solve it in your own wisdom? Or, as Charles Albert Tindley wrote, are you content to "take your burden to the Lord and leave it there"? Why is this an important aspect of trusting Him?

3. Consider the experience of H. G. Spafford. How difficult would it be to feel spiritually whole in the face of such extraordinary loss? How easily is your soul made *unwell* by the anxieties and worries of life?

4. How important is thanksgiving in your prayer life? Make a list of the ways God has blessed your life in answer to prayer—and be reminded of His faithfulness.

CONCLUSION
The Who Is the Why . . .

Arguably the toughest command in the Bible is found in Jesus's words, "Do not worry" (Luke 12:22). Yes, even after all we have seen together, we still end up here with Jesus's challenging words. What are we to do with them?

I haven't looked at a copy of *Mad* magazine in fifty years, but as a boy I read *Mad* on a regular basis. The wry, tongue-in-cheek humor kept me coming back for more, and I must admit that the small book *Mad's Al Jaffee Spews out Snappy Answers to Stupid Questions* taught me a thing or two about the fine art of sarcasm.

But the enduring imagery of *Mad* magazine that I still carry in my mind is that of the iconic cartoon character that symbolized the publication. He was a young man with gapped teeth, freckles, and a vacant stare. Alfred E. Neuman. Why do I mention this? Because Neuman had a life motto that was his consistent response to every problem and every challenge of life. The response? "What, me worry?"

A blanket, one-size-fits-all perspective for anything and everything life could throw at him. "What, me worry?"

Or as a more current proverb from the music world of modern culture would put it, "Don't worry, be happy."

Yes, me worry. (Pardon the grammar.) And when I worry—whether in terms of doubt or anxiety—that worry has follow-on impacts, not the least of which is the fact that worry is one of the greatest thieves of joy we will ever experience.

But hear again Neuman's motto. "What, me worry?" Upon further consideration, I am convinced that *that* is actually where I need to be, but for better reasons. Neuman was always presented as naive at best and simple-minded at worst. I don't want to desist from worrying because of foolish or fraudulent reasons. Yet to be able to honestly affirm that I have no need for worry in my life is a very healthy place to be.

Maybe the best way to respond is by embracing *why* we are urged not to worry. And *who* is urging us. Jesus, the one who came to show us the Father (John 1:18), is challenging us to abandon worry because of who our Father is and how very much He desires to care for us. It would not be amiss to say that your heavenly Father is concerned about everything that you are concerned about. Why? Because if you have trusted Christ as your Savior, He is your Father. As the source of all wisdom, He knows what is best. As the mighty one, He has all power. Not only is this your God—He is your Father! This is a faith-boosting, fear-shattering truth that we need to explore.

In his book *Gifted Hands: The Ben Carson Story*, Dr. Ben Carson wrote:

> "I don't know if I'll get in at Stanford," one premed said to me, after he had sent in his application. "Or anywhere else," he added.
>
> Another mentioned a different school, but the students' worries were essentially the same. I seldom got involved in what I called freaking out, but this kind of talk happened often, especially during our senior year.
>
> One time when this freaking out was going on and I didn't enter in, one of my friends turned to me. "Carson, aren't you worried?"
>
> "No," I said. "I'm going to the University of Michigan Medical School."
>
> "How can you be so sure?"
>
> "It's real simple. My father owns the university."
>
> "Did you hear that?" he yelled at one of the others. "Carson's old man owns the University of Michigan."
>
> Several students were impressed. And understandably, because they came from extremely wealthy homes. Their parents owned great industries. Actually I had been teasing, and maybe it wasn't playing

fair. As a Christian I believe that God—my Heavenly Father—not only created the universe, but He controls it. And, by extension, God owns the University of Michigan and everything else.

I never did explain.

That is the wonder of being God's child! We step into every new day with access to the truth of our God as our Father. Dietrich Bonhoeffer, in *The Cost of Discipleship*, affirmed, "The child asks of the Father whom he knows. Thus the essence of Christian prayer is not general adoration, but definite, concrete petition. The right way to approach God is to stretch out our hands and ask of One who we know has the heart of a Father."

That is the key. The heart of the Father that Jesus has revealed to us is one of care, love, mercy, supply, and provision. Why do we not need to worry? Because of who our Father is! He loves you and you can trust His heart—a fact reinforced by Thomas Chisholm's classic hymn:

> Great is Thy faithfulness, O God my Father,
> There is no shadow of turning with Thee.
> Thou changest not, Thy compassions, they
> fail not;
> As Thou hast been, Thou forever wilt be.
>
> Great is Thy faithfulness!
> Great is Thy faithfulness!
> Morning by morning new mercies I see;

All I have needed Thy hand hath provided.
Great is Thy faithfulness, Lord, unto me!

Because this is the character, trustworthiness, and heart of your God, Jesus can say to you and to me, "Stop worrying." Our God is sufficient. Trust Him.

Spread the Word
by Doing One Thing.

- Give a copy of this book as a gift.
- Share the QR code link via your social media.
- Write a review of this book on your blog, favorite bookseller's website, or at ODB.org/store.
- Recommend this book to your church, small group, or book club.

Connect with us.

Our Daily Bread Publishing
PO Box 3566, Grand Rapids, MI 49501, USA
Email: books@odb.org

Love God. Love Others.

with  **Our Daily Bread.**

Your gift changes lives.

Connect with us. ⨍ ⓞ 𝕐

Our Daily Bread Publishing
PO Box 3566, Grand Rapids, MI 49501, USA
Email: books@odb.org